Mama Is Gonna Take You to the Circus

BEYOND THE DRAMA

UNLOCK THE JOY OF YOUR LIFE'S TRIP

Ameera Almousa

MAMA IS GONNA TAKE YOU TO THE CIRCUS

First published in 2018

ISBN
Print: 978-0-6483403-2-4
Ebook: 978-0-6483403-3-1

Publishing information

Publishing, design and production facilitated
by Passionpreneur Publishing
www.PassionpreneurPublishing.com

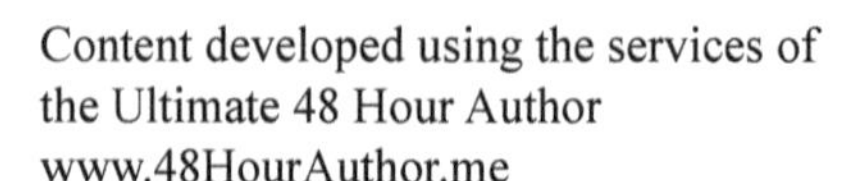
Content developed using the services of
the Ultimate 48 Hour Author
www.48HourAuthor.me

Tel: 1 300 664 006
Diamond Creek
Melbourne, Victoria
Australia 3089

TESTIMONIALS

"Ameera takes you on a journey through life, with its ups and downs, joy and sorrow, challenges and obstacles. Enjoy the journey and let Mama guide you to reach out for the skies."

- Hoda Elsobky
Thinker and Author of
Dare to be Happy.

* * *

"Ameera offers an amazing parable of life as a circus which it is! What a great way to guide the youth about choices in life."

- Moustafa Hamwi
The Passionpreneur

* * *

"Ameera provides a magical connection to life and the excitement of the circus for her readers. 'Mama' helps her young ones tackle life's challenges to soar high—a wonderful journey for us all to reach past the ups and downs of life."

- Nilam Shah
Author of Weighed Down

* * *

"This book is based on real life experiences. Ameera beautifully depicts the different stages in life and correlates it to a circus making it a fun read. Well done. A very impressive read."

- Kay Joosub
Author of Live Deliciously

ABOUT THE AUTHOR

Ameera Almousa, a middle-aged Saudi resident, was raised on traditional family values, amidst some draconian theories surrounding the definition of success.

She aspired to become a young writer. Even though her father was supportive, her talents were confined to the corridors of her University and home. Until recently, she too believed that success meant getting married, being an obedient wife, and raising children.

Ameera successfully completed her Bachelor's degree in Business Administration, and then, like a good daughter, joined the ranks of married women. Her life moved on as expected, but soon, reality struck. She began to believe that she must have a higher calling than just getting married and having children. With one child afflicted with ADHD, she enrolled in some courses to help her child cope with the injustices of life. This triggered a burning desire to achieve more. She was induced to do some soul-searching to identify her real purpose on earth.

To pursue her quest, she enrolled in seminars, attended workshops and became an avid reader on many subjects related to her field of interest, primarily life-coaching and mentoring adolescents so they could withstand and overcome the pressures of their time.

To acquire knowledge and inspiration from experts in her field, Ameera travelled the world and finally realized her true calling—to guide adolescents through her writing. After many years of experience, Ameera is now releasing her first book. Modeled on a trip to the circus, the book provides invaluable tools, guidelines and tutorials on life lessons for both, the young and the old.

AmeeraAlmousa.com

DEDICATION

To my parents, my family, and all those who inspired me to write this book.

Thank you for your unwavering support.

ACKNOWLEDGMENT

To the little girl inside the 5-year-old Ameera sporting a red dress, who always appears during happy times or in places that reflect her spirit. Be it the snowcapped mountains or breezy sea shores, the Ameera who never grew up continues to see the world as full of potential.

To my father, who not only taught me how to read, but also converted me into an avid reader. My father, who taught me that reading opens up a magical world with no boundaries or limitations. The first man who respected me and taught me that there are no gender differences and that limitations are mostly self-imposed.

To my mother, who taught me patience and the art of forgiveness so that I began to see that the feeling of hurt was only transitory.

To my husband, who took me back in time so I was that little girl in the red dress again. My husband, who guided and supported me to achieve my dreams – no matter what they were.

To my big brother, the first person to cheer me on, irrespective of my career choice, who showered me with unconditional love.

To my twin sister; a special thank you for your unwavering support and for taking care of my children during my travels and the times I was away from home. If you hadn't done that, I wouldn't have been able to achieve my objectives in life.

To my other brothers and sisters, who provided me love and support and helped shape my character.

To my six children, for whom I have fun nick names—Mr. Wealth, Miss Adventure, Mr. Knowledge, Mr. Creativity, Little Miss Wisdom and finally, my toddler, Miss Love—where love is the answer to all my life questions. You all are my true inspiration.

To my friends, who did not pressurize me and respected my private time while writing this book, just as they did during my pregnancy.

To Moustafa, who brought back the writer in me.

PREFACE

As a mother of six, I know all too well how difficult it can be growing up, especially in this day and age. Since I myself have been through a lot of challenges growing up, not least because of the fact that I lived in the conservative society of Saudi Arabia, I know how difficult it can be to not just understand the world around you, but also love it for what it is.

As my own childhood was fraught with challenges, I've learnt a lot overcoming them. Due to my extensive experience in this regard, I am well-equipped with the tools to help youths, and even adults, navigate the world's tricky paths.

But while I had the intention of writing this book for quite some time, I did not know exactly how I would go about it. Then, I had an epiphany; the perfect toolbox appeared clear in my mind. I wrote this book using the analogy of a circus. We have all been to a circus, fair or carnival at some point in our life. And even if we haven't, thanks to the proliferation of pop culture, we all have an idea of what they're like.

Thus, using this metaphor is ideal because it allows

me to explain tricky concepts in a way that is easy to understand for everyone. This book will help you understand yourself, others, and the world around you. With its help, you will develop emotional intelligence and will learn how to manage your relationships with other human beings. You will learn how to never lose faith in yourself and stay strong – no matter what. And you will learn how to find it within yourself to work towards becoming the best version of yourself.

You will learn all this within the interesting and fun cover of a circus. So be prepared to be dazzled, because this book is designed to catch your attention just as a circus would.

CONTENTS

INTRODUCTION

Are you ready?

Are you excited?

Do you want to visit the circus?

Hello, I am Mama, and I am here to take you to the circus.

You see, I have set my mind to introduce you to the many marvels and wonders of the circus. You can say, I want to be the magician who pulls out the circus curiosities out of my magic hat. I want to watch as you discover the myriad novelties, to see your eyes widen with wonder and shine brilliantly like the stars. I know how quickly you will learn your way through this circus, especially when you have me, Mama, to help you understand its many quirks and oddities.

As Mama takes you through the circus, and acquaints

you with its many aspects, you will begin to correlate these learnings with your life and its many challenges, and look at them with fresh eyes.

The hat is symbolic of my experiences in life—all that I learned as I walked through the circus on my own, looking at things, admiring both—their strangeness and familiarity. What I really want is to be your guide at the circus—something that I missed out on myself as I was growing up. I sorely felt the lack of direction. You can say this is my way of making amends to my younger self—by guiding the youngsters today who need my help.

When I was young, I had hundreds of questions regarding the circus. No one was there, however, to answer them. So, I had to work my way through the disorientation; I had to learn through trial and error. I gained lessons, but I also lost out on a lot. I don't want young people to lose anything in their circus of life—they should only gain from it. I don't want you all to lose your time, your youth, your money, and your dreams. Let no one tell you to follow the herd—as I was told. Let no one else's passions hijack yours. In this world, which pushes you to become a copy of others, I am here to take you to the circus which only teaches you to be yourself.

I am from Saudi Arabia. The culture here barely permits women to venture out of the security of their homes. It was through sheer determination that I was able to live a more productive life than the one allowed to me by my elders and society. At first, I felt lost, as though abandoned in a maze, without a map. However, I learned. I did that by taking courses at colleges, attending seminars, and burning the midnight oil while my children slept peacefully in their beds.

I dedicated my life to my children—for that is what mothers do. I call myself Mama because I have the same love for all youth as I have for my own children. I am a mother of six. Two of my children are in college, two are teens, and two are under the age of six. I call myself Mama because a mother has unconditional and unquestioning love for her children. She doesn't ask "why?" but "How can I help?" My own mother, who, from the young age of twenty-three, raised seven children, is my inspiration to guide other young people.

The precedent of this book is my house, which I call a circus, because it is open to all teenagers and young adults, related or not, seeking my advice. I love counselling them about finding their direction in life. As I helped those youngsters, I realised that I had also helped their parents in a way. Witnessing the ripple effect of positivity was heart-warming.

I am enthused to reach out and mentor more young people, far and wide. Now, this is my sole purpose in life. Mama can become whoever you want her to be. I can be a toddler with a toddler, or a teen with a teen. My kids see me as an ageless being—just as Mother Nature—for I can transform myself at will to help whoever needs my help.

My son asks me, "Why did you have to wait to realize your dream, Mama?" He is confused as to why I kept putting off my plans. I tell him what is more important is that I am still pursuing those dreams that others did their best to smother. What is more important is that I always kept the flame of my dreams burning. So here I am. I have written this book for you in a language that is not my mother tongue—for my dream is to help you through the life circus.

As I pen these words, I am smiling at the thought that your circus journey will soon begin. I am thinking of the many new paths you will discover, of the many new destinations you will unfold. Soon you will encounter the thrill of the circus and experience its sheer miracle. You will reinvent yourself in the process, for the circus gives you the right tools to do so. You will, as you read on, learn to spread your wings and soar the skies. So it is with this sincere hope and anticipation that I announce: let the amazing circus sojourn begin.

Chapter 1

THE QUEUE

The Day Dawns

The open expanse of the sky is streaked with color. Hues of pastel pink, soft orange, and muted yellow melt over the pale blue heavenly canvas. The long-awaited day has finally arrived. It is almost as if all the elements, the white cotton clouds, the fast rising sun, and the soft breeze, have connived to make this day picture-perfect. Today is the day we go to the circus, finally! There is neither noise, nor any movement. The world is silent and still. Soon, it will stretch its limbs like a giant beast and rise with a mighty yawn, stretching its jaws from the east to the west. As its waking ritual unfolds, all the nooks and crannies will be flooded with sounds and pulsate with life.

The kids are finally waking up. Like little morning

birds, who start chirping to herald the beginning of a new day, I can hear them murmuring to one another. Their little whispers are punctuated by muted cries of excitement and laughter that is quickly muffled. As I am Mama, I understand them better than they understand themselves. I can paint a picture with my eyes closed, based on the soundscape. One child moves his mouth rapidly as the words seem to tumble over one another. The other child covers his mouth with his tiny hand to muffle the easy laughter, that spills out anyway, as the third watches from a distance, rubbing both eyes, to will the remnants of sleep away.

Their waking up sounds elevate my spirits as I look forward to the day about to unfold. I look forward to the happiness my children will experience and the lessons they will learn today, for this is the day I have been anticipating with a shared eagerness and excitement.

And So It Starts

We have somewhere to go today. Our eyes are brimming with hope and enthusiasm. This is a day, unlike other days. I wonder if it is a mere projection of our own feelings or if the world actually appears to be brighter, sharper, and more vivid than it did just yesterday, or the day before. This happens, though, does it not? Our mood takes on a life of its own and proceeds to color the whole world in its own hues. That is what has transpired today, I am sure. We are feeling so cheerful and upbeat that the world itself seems to respond in kind, by being sunny and bright. We get ready for our upcoming excursion with enthusiasm.

Our small vehicle seems cramped, with so many of us piling in. But, today, there is enough room in our hearts to accommodate each other comfortably, without any complaints. Earlier journeys were marked with discord every now and then, but not today. Today's journey is happy and peaceful; no elbowing and jostling one another for leg space. We ignore the cacophony from the road and the agitated crowds as we set our eyes on our destination. We know that today, we will learn about the path of life, and how to unlock its joys.

We Arrive On Time

Are you excited?

We have arrived at the circus.

As we join the crowd that surges forward like the rising and unstoppable waves of the ocean, we feel as if we are all one. We feel curiously connected as our concerns, fears, and motivations in life, appear to be the same. Paradoxically, the crowd gives us anonymity and individuality, but also embraces us as if we were its long-lost children. Making our way through the noisy and animated throng, we walk jauntily, like goats traversing precipitous mountain terrain with ease and aplomb.

Though you may not be accustomed to it—in fact, you may never have been here before in your lives—you will find yourselves embracing the reigning spirit of gaiety with the openness that only children are capable of. As you watch the animated faces around, hear snippets of their eager conversations, see them laugh out loud in excitement, you feel you fit right in. The robe of happiness and joy, which may even be termed as the uniform feature of the circus, befits you.

Finally, we see the bright, twinkling lights of the circus. On and off the little lights blink as if to tease us with the promise of all that the circus has in store for us. The morning breeze flows gently over us, bringing with it a whiff of hot candy and stale popcorn as well as the smell that is peculiar to large gatherings. The inimitable sounds of the circus keep getting louder till we feel as if we are in the middle of an action film, with its exciting twists and turns. I hold my children's hands, our hearts beating in tandem with the collective heart of the energetic crowd that has come to witness the circus.

The Queue

Mama is here as you line up in the queue of the circus. My job as Mama is to escort you through this circus in a way that will make you grow in terms of your self-awareness and self-reliance.

Now, you are in the queue to the ticket booth and the line stretches endlessly ahead of you. There are people before you and there are people behind you. You stand there and await your turn to get to the front of the line and procure your own ticket to the circus. Mama is also excited to impart the wisdom she has gleaned from years of experience.

So what is a queue? By definition, a queue is a line waiting to be processed or it is a sequence of people or vehicles waiting for their turn to be attended to. As you may already have inferred, a queue involves waiting. And waiting demands patience. Now, people may get the idea that patience is all about the quantity of time, measurable in minutes, spent waiting. However, patience is not as much about the quantity of time, as it is about its quality.

As Joyce Meyer said, "Patience is not simply the ability to wait, it is how we behave while we're waiting."

Most of us, in the course of our day-to-day lives, have to wait in queues. Queues are simply unavoidable. Be it waiting in line at the bank or lining up in front of the coffee counter; queuing up remains a part of everyone's life. You have to wait for your turn. You need to understand one other thing as well; queues are not just literal, but can be metaphorical in nature too. Think of the various queues you are in at this point in your life. You may be in queue at school or college, waiting to graduate. Or in your professional career, waiting for a promotion; conversely, you might be unemployed, and in a queue for a job.

What Is Your Queue?

Stop for a minute and identify your queue or queues. Once you have done that, label your queue accordingly. You can be in the "student queue," "college queue" and so on. Then, make it a point to acknowledge the queue that you currently occupy. Accept and own your current status. I say this because if you refuse to accept the queue you are in right now, you might endanger your chance of smoothly transitioning to the next queue of your life. Yes, there are more queues to follow and you must prepare yourself to find and occupy the correct queue when the time comes.

This can be better explained by an example. Suppose you are a student attending school. You are, then, in the "student queue." Your worries are the same as the worries of your peers and just like them, you look forward to jumping to the next queue when the time is right. Now, you are waiting in the queue patiently. As Mama said earlier, patience is about how you wait when standing in line.

So, let's take an overview of the way you wait and how you spend your time in the student queue. Do you concentrate more on your studies or on play? Is your life characteristic of a student's life? Mama can suggest some things that you can add to your routine to improve the quality of waiting in the queue. You can try going to the library, making a study schedule and sticking to it, and not overspending from your student budget.

Also, check out your wardrobe. Do your clothes reflect your student status? If not, assess the situation critically. Once you are done reflecting, assemble a wardrobe that matches your current queue in life. Dress like a student but also make sure that your personality shines through your appearance. I say this to emphasize that your individuality is important. Do not follow the herd blindly. Use accessories that reveal a little bit of who you are. Add a dash of color to your appearance. The point is to maintain your distinct style and carry yourself in a manner that not only befits you as a student, but that also makes your queue time more fruitful.

Is This The Right Queue?

As you wait in your queue in life, you might end up wondering, "Am I even standing in the right queue?" You might lose your sense of direction and end up in the wrong queue due to genuine confusion or because you made the mistake of following others instead of following your own heart.

Do you find yourself pleasing others to the extent that you replace your dreams and goals with their goals and dreams? These others may be your friends or family; people who influence you or whom you admire and wish to emulate. So, should others decide your future or should you take charge of your own life?

The fact is that everyone has their own dreams and desires, in much the same way that all have their own distinct destinies. I would go so far as to say that your dreams are part of your genetic makeup, which is unique and particular to you alone. Think of your fingerprint; isn't it all yours, and in a way that no one can ever hope to replicate or reproduce? You, likewise, are one of a kind. The same should be the case with your dreams. I say this because I want you to examine yourself and your dreams.

Are your dreams your own or are they somebody else's dreams that are imposed on you, from within or externally? If, for example, you assume the dreams of your friends as your own, stop and ask yourself; do you want to live the life that they want to? Or are your aspirations different from theirs? It is time you realise that you are your own person with your own, highly individual set of dreams and goals. Once you do that, you will become an agent in your life rather than a mere spectator.

Here, Mama will give you this advice; regardless of the queue you are in currently, just follow your passion. Mama says this because people often let others dictate the terms in their lives, and then end up being dissatisfied and unhappy. For example, if you are a student, you might let your friends make the choice of which field you should pursue at university. How can you be satisfied with the choice that others have made for you? What about your own interests and passions? After all, others don't know your heart like you do, be they friends or family.

Mama wants you to take control of your own life. Think of it as a car that you and only you should drive because you are the only one who knows the routes as well as the destination. If you let people, who are clueless about the directions or your destination, take charge, then who else can you blame but yourself? Carefully plan the next queue in your life; select one that will reflect your passions and be in line with your true calling.

Make the correct decisions in the first place for this will take you to your final goal. Additionally, it will improve your decision-making skills. You will also learn to trust yourself in the process. This is how you can make the best of the queue that you are in currently. Make productive use of your time by becoming more self-assured and focused. You will find deep reserves of resources within yourself, which will help you overcome any and all obstacles successfully. Own your queue and make decisions keeping the present, as well as the future, in mind. You are a wonder in the making. The way you live your time in your current queue will set the foundation for the success of the future queues you will occupy.

What To Do When In A Queue

People spend their time in a queue differently. Even though they may be standing in the same queue, their behavior is markedly different from one another. This is obvious because everyone is unique. Each one has inherent peculiarities, preferences, quirks, fears and motivations; naturally their conduct in queues reflects who they are as individuals.

Take the example of two colleagues going on a trip abroad. Now, for all intents and purposes, their queue is the same. They are both in the same "professional queue," yet their behaviors differ. While one of the two might like to prepare fully before departing on a trip, the other might board the plane with half-baked preparations. While one doesn't mind waking up early to reach the airport well before time, the other might sleep in late, desirous of starting the journey with a fresh mind and rested body.

While one arrives two hours early, the other manages to make it just five minutes before boarding time.

Here, it is important to note that neither of these preferred behaviours can be labelled as bad. There simply is no good or bad behavior when in a queue. However, people may need to modify their lifestyle to match the demands of the queue. The point to take away is that everyone must be given the respect they deserve without any discrimination. Learn from all types of people to improve yourself as an individual. All learning comes in handy and nothing you learn will ever go to waste.

It Is Good To Watch The Crowded Queue

You are back in the circus queue with people before

you and people behind you. Imagine this is what you see as you wait in line: some people shuffle their feet in frustration, some swing their arms restlessly, some spend their time chattering, while others wait patiently, observing the multitude of strangers around, with their own, unknown, life stories.

Do you want to know their stories? Do you find yourself interested or are you apathetic? Do you watch others with curiosity, willing to listen to their tales and seethings from a new perspective?

Amidst all the bustle, you unconsciously learn new things. As you talk to strangers, you absorb the wisdom that they have collected over the years. You find yourself growing, as you not only learn, but also unlearn.

You learn to smile at others. You learn the best time to join the queue and you learn when to avoid it. As you practice watching others, you learn some crucial lessons on how to have a good time at the circus. People might advise you on the best time to arrive, the best time to leave, the best shows to watch, the best food to eat and what to avoid. The lessons you learn will guide you to make the right decisions.

From others' experiences as well as from your own, you will also learn how to budget your trip and account for unforeseen expenses, maximizing your time at the circus.

Let Mama explain this through an example. Suppose you came to the circus eager to watch the contortionist. You wanted to see them twist their bodies into unfathomable shapes, and wondered if they could really fit themselves into a small box and bend their bodies backwards so that their heads ended up between their legs. You were fascinated by what seemed impossible to you from the comfort of your home.

However, when you arrive at the circus, you find out that a show on escapology is scheduled at the same time as the contortionists' show. Though you were not even aware of a show called escapology before, you suddenly find yourself extremely curious. You have to make a quick decision—contortionist or escapology. You are more inclined to opt for escapology, to see people escape from chains, boxes, straitjackets, and locked containers successfully. However, there is one problem: the ticket to escapology costs more than the ticket to the contortionist's show. What do you do now? Give up the opportunity to watch a show you desperately want to attend? You could have avoided this dilemma before coming to the circus if only you had planned for such eventualities.

This is why, earlier, Mama emphasized the need to be prepared in terms of budget, as well as time. Here, you learn the essential lesson that provisions should be made in terms of time to be spent and money to be expended beforehand. So, always make it a point to anticipate emergencies and sudden changes in the plan to avoid feeling disappointed with your experience and compromising on your fun. The ultimate goal of coming to the circus is to have a good time and create lasting good memories. Preparation for exigencies will ensure that your good time isn't marred by let-downs.

Time For Yourself

As you stand in the queue, you familiarize yourself with the people around you and the surroundings. You might have come to the circus on your own or with family. Either way, you can use this opportunity to grow positively as an individual. When with others, you will learn how to improve the quality of your collective experience in the queue and in the circus. When on your own, you will become more self-aware and find ways to make better choices when selecting future queues.

Your decision to go to the circus on your own should be based on your own passion. When one stands alone in any queue, there is always a reason for it. Have you stopped to ask yourself your own reasons? You may be in a strange land, with no friends or family to accompany you. Or you may have been desirous to experience the circus alone. The point is to acknowledge your reasons for being at the circus and for being there alone. Once you do that, you will find out more about your own choices. You will accept who you are and what you want. As a result, you will find yourself more engaged with life and more enthusiastic to live it.

As you spend time at the circus with your family, you will recall all the positive emotions and expectations associated with this experience. How the day seemed brighter and your spirits lighter as you started out. Accordingly, you will endeavour to preserve those optimistic and positive feelings. You will want to share those feelings with your companions. To ensure that this experience lives up to expectations, your own and of those who have accompanied you, some steps will need to be taken. Once you take those steps, you will learn how to get along with your own family, how to become more considerate towards them and how to take care of their needs so that they, and by extension, you, are happy.

You will show concern for the well-being of your family and be considerate towards their needs. You might ask, "Do you want to watch the juggler or the lion tamer?" or, "Do you want to have dinner before leaving?" They will be touched by your sincerity and reciprocate. You will bond with each other and create happy memories together that will last long after this trip has ended. In this way, your time at the circus will have been used productively.

How Prepared Are You?

Did you come to the circus prepared or did you come here without any plans? Did you consider how the presence or absence of a good plan would determine the quality of your experience at the circus? Did you take care of your personal needs for waiting in the queue and for watching the different shows, or did you shrug it off as just another regular day that you did not need to prepare for? All the questions are relevant as they can decide the course that your day will take. Whether the day will be a raging success or a total failure.

So, think first of your practical needs. Did you wear the right shoes and the right clothes for the circus? This is important because whether or not you are comfortable in your own skin will directly influence the experience you will have today. This applies to your experiences in real life and the queues that you currently occupy. Are you comfortable as you occupy your student or professional queue? If not, you need to rethink your strategy in life so that you can attract good rather than bad experiences.

When coming to the circus, did you follow a map that would help you navigate your way? Or did you hope to find your way as you went along? Which of these two options do you think is better if you want to have a fun experience, unmarred by mishaps and accidents? It would not do to get lost on the way because that would mean wasted time and energy and cost you the good time you could have had at the circus.

This applies to your life too. Do you have a road map to your future? Do you have a blueprint for achieving the goals that you have set for yourself? Or is it acceptable to you to lose your way in life and end up where you never wanted to be in the first place?

These are questions you should ask yourself. When you do that, you will find you need to work on your future plans to ensure a good life. You need to focus on a central goal and then make plans accordingly. Anything that would detract from making your future amazing must be eliminated. Conversely, everything that will enhance your life experiences, inducing joy and satisfaction, must be added to your life plans.

Do Not Use Your Phone In The Queue

As someone who lives in the modern world with its latest technologies, you may find it hard to unplug yourself from the many devices that you own, primarily your mobile phone. A mobile used to be a happy convenience, but today, mobile phones are the reason you are disconnected, rather than connected to people. Every second, you are inundated with innumerable notifications like, "New text message!" or "10 New WhatsApp Messages!" or "The Biggest Pizza Deal of the Month" or "So-and-So Has Sent You a Friend Request!"

The bottom line is you need to unplug yourself from your phone when you come to the circus. This is to ensure that you take out quality time for yourself, undisturbed by interruptions, and in tune with your surroundings and the related experiences. This will ensure that you connect with people, hear their stories and tell them yours.

By switching off your phone, you ensure that you have real experiences instead of virtual ones where you watch things from the barrier of the screen. If you want and value meaningful exchanges with people in life, be they your family, friends or strangers like those who are in the queue with you, you need to set your priorities straight. You need to decide what is more important for you, the real world with its real people or the make-believe world of your smartphone.

Once you unplug yourself from your phone, you will start noticing the beauty of the world that surrounds you. You will be able to use your senses as God intended them to be used. To see, hear, and smell the pleasant environment. You might even strike up friendships with strangers, and be influenced by their vivaciousness and verve for life. This will be a valuable experience for you, even if you never see those strangers again. You will proactively make the conscious choice of living in the moment. No longer will you feel compelled to fulfil other people's expectations of you. And no longer will you hunger for their approval. At the circus, you will realize that their expectations and approval or disapproval matter less than your self-approval. You will learn to live for yourself and so, become a more satisfied and happy person whom others would love to be around. Meeting new people and having meaningful interactions with them will enrich your life in ways you could not have predicted. You will soon become a better, happier version of yourself.

What Is The Reason For Going To The Circus?

You came to the circus for one reason only: to have a good time. You wanted to feel happy, you welcomed the excitement of the plan, and you looked forward to creating new memories. When at the circus, you ensured that you and your companions had a fun experience.

You saw sights that you would remember for the rest of your life. You watched fascinating shows where unbelievable feats were performed. Do not hesitate to express your appreciation for those people who prepared so hard to perform for you at the circus. Take a look at the festive scene and absorb the sights and the sounds of the circus, for this celebration of the human spirit will soon come to an end. Engrave your experience in your heart, for in the future, you will reminisce about the circus and regret that it ended too soon.

And so it is with life. The good times are like the ones spent at the circus. Enjoy them while they last so that the happiness you experience can linger for a while. If, despite hurdles and obstacles, your time spent is one that you will cherish for long, you have fulfilled your purpose of coming to the circus. You have met new people, forged new friendships, learned from them and enhanced your own personality. If you have become a better person in the process, then your mission has been accomplished. Revel in your success for it is hard-earned and well-deserved.

It Has Only Just Begun

Mama, hopefully, has taught you some valuable life lessons so far, because the circus is about to begin. She wishes that you have a great time. Identifying and naming your queue was the first step. Then taking time out to make it your own was the second. Learning your priorities and getting them straight was yet another step. Now, Mama believes that you are prepared to take on what is coming your way next.

You need to remember one thing as you go along and immerse yourself fully in this experience: you need to give of yourself as much as you ask from the circus, to make the best of it. This may seem tough, but Mama will take your hand and guide you through the circus.

She will make sure that you are never alone and never without direction. If you lose your way, Mama will come to your rescue. In short, Mama will be your compass, your guide and your friend, all in one. Remember, there are lessons to be learnt, but there is also a lot of fun to be had. The time of your life awaits you. Now, if you respond to it being true to yourself, the exuberance of the circus will envelop you in its arms. Trust Mama when she says that this is the beginning of a good time for you.

Chapter 2

THE CLOWN

The Circus Begins

After the wait in the queue, you finally get to the ticket booth where you purchase your entrance pass to the circus. You clutch the ticket in your hand, happy to be one of the circus-goers on this day.

Your wait in the queue has paid off and now, you head towards your destination—the one you have been looking forward to. The usher collects the ticket from you and steers you in, right behind the rest of the crowd. As you head in, you are greeted by the diverse sounds of the circus: the pattering feet of little children, excitedly running from one amusing spectacle to another, the squeals of carefree laughter, the sounds of the squeaking carousel, the whoosh of the high-velocity roller coaster, and the shrill screams of those riding in the Ferris wheel.

Your experience in the circus has just begun. As you look around with wonder in your eyes, who is the person who almost instantly draws your eye? In the sea of attractions that surrounds you, who is the one person to have caught your attention?

It is the Circus Clown.

There are a hundred wonders for the eye to witness and absorb at the circus; the glaring neon name boards, the fairy lights looped around the many tents, lending the whole place a dreamlike ambience, the jingles and choruses that only get louder as you go deeper into the circus, and the mouth-watering aromas of circus food drifting towards you, making your experience a highly sensory one. The circus air holds a promise of exciting things in store for you.

However, in all the hubbub, the clown retains a place of prominence. He is the circus celebrity. In fact, can you even think of a circus without thinking of the clown at the same time? Aren't the two synonymous in your mind? The circus experience cannot be detached from the figure of the clown, greeting people merrily, like long-lost friends. You have never met the clown before, yet he is instantly recognizable and familiar, as if you, too, have known him all your life.

Have you ever wondered who the clown is? How he exists before and beyond the moments you see him? Do you think of the clown's history and his future? Do you ever wonder what the clown is when he is not a clown? Have you ever thought of the preparations made before a clown manifests in his form, before you.

If you assert your mind and draw parallels, you will realise that the clown, in truth, can be considered a representation of yourself, in the same way that the circus is a metaphor for your life.

The Clown

As if drawn by some invisible magnetic force, your eyes go straight to the clown. He stands out. He is one of a kind. You cannot mistake him for anyone else, ever. Even if you have never been to the circus before, you would know a clown when you see one. Why do you think that happens? Why do you think the clown is not subsumed by the crowd but is distinct and distinguishable? There are so many aspects that set a clown apart. Instantly familiar though he may be, I am pretty sure that most people never stop to really look behind the clown's exterior to truly appreciate what he is and all that he represents.

Do you know what a clown alley is? It is the place where the clown dresses up, puts paint and makeup on, and equips himself with the props that would help him entertain you. The clown alley, then, is the place where the clown conducts his preparation for his circus routine. In our circus experience, we never pause to think about what the clown does backstage, the motions that he goes through to put on his best face for us, and the mental processes that assist him in becoming, without question, an integral part of the circus.

Imagine the clown putting his rainbow colored wig on. Visualize how he powders his face all white and then spreads the white base over his neck and chest. Then, imagine how he paints his eyebrows thick. He applies makeup to his eyelids so they pop out. Later, he adds a vibrant dash of red to his appearance, coating his mouth in a wide, bright smile that he knows, will bring smiles to the faces of many. Then he puts on his clothes that are colorful and cheerful—white frilled collars, blue, yellow, and green striped socks, polka-dotted shirt, and a bright red jumpsuit that he pulls over. He finishes off by putting on his exaggerated shoes and finally, his red clown nose. The getup is complete. Before your very eyes, a new person emerges, one who has transformed into someone you know as the circus clown.

The change is astounding, if you think about it. In a matter of minutes, a person, who earlier looked like an ordinary person, evolves into a novel being. Breaking out of a homogenous mass of humanity, this person becomes someone who stands out, who does not blend, and who is one of a kind—the circus clown! This process of transformation, though not very lengthy, is impactful enough to make a world of difference.

Why do you think the clown goes through all the trouble to put on this exterior? What allures him to become an entertainer who makes a fool of himself in front of a crowd of hundreds? It is, very simply, the clown's wish which is two-fold in nature. The clown wants to be unique, and he does become unique by donning this persona. Also, the clown wants to make others happy, which he does, as you will see in the circus; there is nowhere that the clown will go where he won't put a smile on people's faces or get a laugh out of them. To make people smile, the clown will not even stop short at pulling a sad face. In his desire to spread happiness, the clown will work hard and endure discomfort happily, because for him bringing smiles to people's faces is a meaningful act.

But What About You?

In the circus of life, you can be many things all at once. First, you thought of life as waiting in the queue. Now, I will ask you to think of yourself as the circus clown. In fact, the more you read of this circus journey of life, the more you will realize that you, in effect, are the clown in the circus of your life. How does it feel to be the main attraction?

To help you understand the parallels I have drawn, I shall ask you to trace the similarities that exist between your life experiences and a clown's experiences at the circus. When you undertake this small task that I have just asked, you are more likely to end up realizing that there aren't similarities at all! So now, I will ask you to identify the dissimilarities.

Do you, as you begin your day, prepare to greet it in the same way that a clown prepares to greet the visitors at the circus? Do you take the time to put on your best face? Do you open your heart to the positive things in life instead of absorbing the negativity that the world may dole out?

Let me pare it down to basics for you. As you begin your day, do you wake up with a mentality geared to make the best of that day? Do you smile in anticipation when you open your eyes? Or do you frown in consternation and dread? Do you feel your own self-worth and value or do you allow self-criticism and self-hate to pull you down? I pose these questions to you so you can ask these questions of yourself. Take time out to analyse your inner landscape, your inner being. Now, tell me, how well acquainted are you with your own heart?

As you get out of bed and prepare for the day, do the external trappings that you put on reflect the inner you? Does the façade you have taken on align with what lies within you? How much time do you really take to get ready? How much attention are you willing to pay to yourself? Are you fine imitating others and looking the way they look or do you want to be your own self? Is your outward appearance in line with who you really are?

In reality, if you are not in touch with yourself, you may end up creating a false appearance. If you are unaware of who you are or if you are unwilling to accept yourself, there will be a fundamental disconnect in your life. This disconnect or detachment that you have with yourself will most definitely manifest in your outer appearance. Thus, instead of following your own heart, you might try to pretend to be someone else. You may style your hair or clothes to imitate your favourite celebrity, thereby reflecting who they are, not who you are.

If this is the case, all your efforts will be targeted towards adopting pretenses rather than towards enhancing your own God-given talents and characteristics. In your attempt to put on a charade, you may pretend to have a perfect life, in front of friends and peers. You might wear a constant smile and not allow a single frown of worry to knit your brow in the course of your day. However, on the inside you might be suffering more than anyone could ever guess. The disconnection, you see, will be quite real and will eventually take a toll on you.

When that happens, the façade that you have built, maybe over a course of several years, will crack. You will be left questioning yourself. Before you get to that unfortunate point that several people do in life, you need to be aware of the way out. The fact is that the world today prizes conformity over everything else. Due to peer pressure of familial or social expectations, you might have been forced to give up your real self. The herd mentality that prevails in modern society divests you of your individuality, of the very things that make you who you are. Many people with immense potential end up being mere copies of the standards that the world has seen fit to impose on everyone.

So, how can you break out of this mould that you might, even at the present moment, be forced to occupy? I can give you a very simple answer to that question—by being the circus clown of the circus that is life.

This is not intended to make you laugh, no. This is intended to be a prompt for you to consider what the circus clown does every single day that he shows up at the circus. As explained earlier, the clown takes time in the clown alley to dress up before he confronts the world that visits the circus. Brave and fearless, he prepares himself in a way that he feels is right. His outward appearance is not made to fit in; it is made to stand out.

So should be your modus operandi in life. Do not try to be one of the crowd, but be courageous enough to be your extraordinary self, just like the circus clown.

Be Yourself

In a world full of copies and reproductions, be yourself. This will lend authenticity and sincerity to your outer appearance and will be more effective than copying anyone else. No longer will you have to feel as if you were living someone else's life or worse, your own life but in someone else's shoes! Give yourself the time that you deserve. For that, first you have to understand and accept yourself. In other words, before you embrace the world, you have to embrace yourself.

You seek a world of color outside. At the circus, you will see that. However, to be a part of that circus—that is your life—instead of standing on the sidelines like a mere observer, you need to approach things with the right attitude and the right preparation. To embrace a life that is full of colors, you must first look in the mirror and recognize yourself.

Yes, you will have your scars: fears and failures that may prevent you from going down the roads that you want to follow. However, you have your motivations and ambitions that are uniquely yours. These must take center stage in your life. If you allow them to, they will drive you to your destination–the one where you really want to go instead of where others may be trying to push you. The best way to ensure that you take the road that you want in life is to find out who you are. This will necessarily entail discovering what you really desire from life.

When you find out your purpose as well as your strengths and weaknesses, you can take the first step towards the right goals. You will have to work on your qualities, the ones that you possess and which are distinctively and exclusively yours, so that they shine. Just like the circus clown, work for the purpose that you find meaningful and satisfying. It would mean standing out, but do not be hesitant. It is only fair that the limelight of your life is on you and not on anybody else.

The Mirror

"The mirror is my best friend, because when I cry it never laughs."
- Charlie Chaplin

As I told you earlier, life may render you disconnected from your own self. There might come a period when you are unable to identify your true self. However, as you go down the circus of life, you will also undergo the process of rediscovery, albeit only if you arm yourself with the right tools. Here, I would share a poem with you that I find uplifting and motivating in the hope that you will too. It is by Nobel Prize-winning, Saint Lucian poet, Derek Walcott, titled 'Love After Love':

The time will come
when, with elation
you will greet yourself arriving
at your own door, in your own mirror
and each will smile at the other's welcome,
and say, sit here. Eat. You will love again the
stranger who was your self.
Give wine. Give bread. Give back your heart
to itself, to the stranger who has loved you
all your life, whom you ignored for another,
who knows you by heart.
Take down the love letters from the bookshelf,
the photographs, the desperate notes,
peel your own image from the mirror.
Sit. Feast on your life.

As Walcott put it so eloquently, self-love can be the most transformative feeling to ever experience. When you accept who you are—not just accept, but embrace yourself—you will find yourself opening up to live life and to experience life's circus fully. To turn your back on yourself, to disregard your own feelings and emotions, and to live life as a spectator and not a participant, can rob you of the happiness that you deserve. Once you are finally able to see things as they are—and yourself, more importantly—without any warped filters of expectations blocking your vision, you will be able to find your true purpose in life. As you do that, you will enter the right queue with the right attitude. Later, just like the circus clown, you will be the star of your own circus.

Your Morning Can Make Your Day

Invest time in yourself. Develop a morning ritual that will set the right tone for the rest of your day. Remember, if you start your day right, it will have greater chances of going right throughout. The right intentions and attitude will take you a long way. So, plan your day in the right way from the start. Your morning ritual should be full of positivity so that the theme of your day is put into place.

If you are positive, you will not just give out but attract positive vibes. Conversely, if you give in to pessimism, the same will come looking for you no matter where you go. The correct approach can make a big difference. Take your mornings as the time to prepare to be the best that you can be on a particular day. Think of the room where you get ready for the day as the clown alley that you have all to yourself. Before facing the day, you must put on the armour that will help you navigate the world in the most productive way possible.

Just as the clown painstakingly enhances his traits, so must you, though not in the physical sense, as the clown does. You don't need to put on a wig, a mask, makeup, and a fake nose. You don't need to wear clothes that are too bright. What you do have to undergo, however, is a process whereby you prepare to be the center. Put a smile on your face so that your whole body radiates positivity. Make positivity the habit of your life.

Then, follow some practical steps for optimism to take root in you. Look up at the sky. Listen to the birds chirping. As you raise your eyes to the morning sun which shines bright, you will realize that no one can bring you down. With your head held high, you will be able to ignore the petty issues that draw your attention away from the things that truly count. Appreciate the blue of the sky, the orange of the sun, the green of the trees and the red of the flowers. Allow all the colors to suffuse your vision.

Soak in the sounds as you wake up—birds chirping, the one or two lone cars that might race down the street below, the footsteps of your family members as they, too, wake up to greet the day. Take all those sounds in and use them as background music for the rest of your day. Eat and drink what you enjoy. Breathe the fresh air and smell the faint scent of flowers pervading the air. Wear your favorite clothes that match the weather so that you are comfortable and happy all through the day.

Allow your inner self to unfold by picking up the signals of positivity that the world sends your way. Don't be impatient. It may take some time before you accustom yourself to truly enjoy the beauty around you and to be optimistic as you face a new day. However, allow serenity into your life. Be hopeful and expect good things to happen to you. It is only when you become receptive to the good that is in the world instead of resisting it, that good things will come your way. Read motivational material so that your spirits are elevated and you are prepared to meet the day with your heart and mind at peace. Cheer yourself up because you are the one who is best at that job!

In all that you do, always remember that everyone around you has their own story. Learn from the clown of the circus to appreciate everyone's struggles and to listen to everyone's tales. Make it a point to pay attention to people. You should not only respect the clown for all that he does for people but also adopt his message as your own—the message of spreading happiness, positivity and joy to people and first of all, to yourself. Open your eyes wide to truly see people. Make others happy for the happiness you send out will always find a way back to you in one form or another. Sometimes, even a smile sent in someone's direction can do wonders. Remember, this is your one chance to experience the circus of life so, enjoy it while it lasts. In the words of **Charlie Chaplin**,

> *"Life is a play that does not allow resting, so sing, cry, dance, laugh, and live intensely before the curtains close, and the play ends with no applause."*

Seize The Day

Mama hopes that as you read this chapter, you thought deeply about the circus clown, and were able to put yourself in his place. You were able to learn a few things. The clown communicates with the audience through gestures and pantomime—he renders verbal language superfluous. Do you know what that means? It means that the magical influence of the clown cannot be restricted; in fact, the clown exudes positivity and builds an instant rapport with the audience, all without depending on words. His communication with people is very strong—and this is because the clown is not distracted but is fully in the moment. Mama hopes you have learnt a crucial life lesson; being fully present is essential if you want to live life to the fullest.

The world today runs on clicks, demands instant gratification, and is driven by short attention spans. People concentrate not on living but on recording the moment. How many times have you watched a beautiful sunset, or attended a fun party, only to have your phone held out in your hand, busily snapping pictures? In the frenzy of taking the perfect picture to freeze the moment, you forget to live things as they unfold right before your eyes. You don't notice and absorb the beauty that surrounds you. You become a detached bystander rather than someone who is in the moment.

You might store those pictures in the memory card of your computer, thinking you will retrieve them at a later date, and probably never look at them again. However, if you had stored the moment in the database of your memory, it would be much more meaningful and long-lasting. Try being present and living in the moment as you experience the circus, just like the circus clown. Forget about taking picture after picture to look back on and reminisce. Be yourself and let others be themselves. Do not be absent from the present moment and let go of being judgmental towards others; only when you do so, will you begin to understand the profundity of things around you.

Practice silence, just like the clown. There are other, better ways to communicate and connect. Explore those alternate avenues of interaction and focus on the present that is yours, not on the future that may never arrive, at least not in the way that you currently envisage or predict. Make each moment of your day come alive by existing in it wholly, without any anxieties of what may come. The day is all yours to seize.

Chapter 3

THE ACROBAT

The Big Red Circus Tent

You are in the big red circus tent now, along with a huge crowd. The roof is quite high, supported by tall masts. The circus ring lies before you and a tier of seats occupied by rows of people. Everyone has come to the circus for the same purpose as you. Yet, everyone will take different things from this seemingly universal experience. You feel bombarded by the choices of shows available for your entertainment. However, Mama believes that, by now, you have understood that there is more to this circus than mere entertainment. The circus is a repository of wisdom and knowledge for you and as you struggle to make sense of it, Mama is right here to help you along.

The shows about to be performed will mesmerize

you; there is no doubt about that. But before you are bedazzled by the circus acts, you need to make a resolution: while you appreciate the beauty of the performance, you will also notice the skill of the performers and their hard work. More importantly, you will look beneath the glittery surface and examine the circus performance deeply. It is all about your life, after all—you only need to approach it with the right perspective.

Vantage Point

The show is about to start. You have taken your seat in front of the circus ring where the performers are setting the stage for the amazing acts that will unfold before your eyes. However, have you stopped to assess how good your view of the performance is? Do you occupy the vantage position? Is your seat strategically placed to afford you an unobstructed view of the show? Here, Mama will give you one piece of critical advice: when in the circus tent, always ensure that you have a clear and unhindered view. This is crucial if you want to experience the circus without missing anything of importance.

Perspective, or the way you look at things, is often more important than the thing itself. How is that so? It is because a balanced perspective is what consolidates a balanced worldview. So, for you, it is essential to maintain a fair and stable standpoint before you make up your mind about any issue. You need to make sure that you have all the facts and that you have them straight. The only way you make sound decisions and reach correct conclusions is if you are an informed person.

Being a well-informed and knowledgeable individual will ensure that the decisions you take in life are not biased or based on unverified assumptions. Now, before learning about things that are external to you, you must strive to be aware of yourself. In the preceding chapter, Mama told you of the significance of self-awareness and self-acceptance. So, apply what you learnt earlier in your life as you proceed. Once you know yourself, you can move on to understanding other people and situations around you. Empowered with the right information, you can make wise decisions yourself without allowing others to control your future.

From your vantage point, you will have full view of the events that unfold. As you watch things happen in real time, you will be equipped with all the necessary information before you proceed to form an opinion, pass judgement, or pronounce your verdict. Once you have processed the available information, ask questions to clear doubts or have a deeper understanding.

Once you make this a habit, you can reap the advantages of being an informed person. Your erudition will become a shield that will stop other people's assumptions and biases from corrupting and influencing you, from driving the decisions that you take in your life. You will learn that while taking advice from those wiser than yourself is good, it is important for you to exercise your own intellect. Your intellectual faculty has to be supported by the information that you gather from your surroundings, relying on your God-given senses. Once you are in that sought-after vantage position, you can sit back and watch as the acrobat appears in the circus ring. It is the acrobat's turn to entertain and inform you.

The Acrobat

Who is the acrobat?

Have you ever pondered over the quintessential qualities that make an acrobat who he is? They are balanced, agile, coordinated, and have strong spatial orientation. The acrobat would not be performing in the circus ring before you if he had not honed these skills that many are born with or acquire in life. Most of us never attempt to recognize that the dexterity of the acrobat can be ours too, if we choose. Now, this dexterity is both physical and mental; it is of the literal as well as metaphorical kind. The acrobat, then, is a metaphor for you. He will teach you some valuable life lessons like how to handle the conundrums of life.

The acrobat is very much in touch with his physicality. You will attest to this fact as you, in awe, observe the acrobat perform physical feats that you couldn't even imagine. You might watch him walk across a tightrope, as if gravity didn't exist for him. You might wonder, wide-eyed, that the daring acrobat on the flying trapeze who swings from one fly bar to another, is gifted in ways that you are not. However, nothing could be further from the truth. As Mama said earlier, the acrobat is a representation of yourself.

Even so, you cannot help but be awe-struck and hypnotized by the acrobat. Right now, you cannot think of the similarities between you and him; and you might not, at present, be capable of learning things from the acrobat. This is because, in this moment, as the acrobat demonstrates his amazing skills, you can do nothing but watch. Lessons will come later as I ask you to process the sights that you saw.

In the present moment, you are awe-struck as you watch the jaw-dropping feats performed. At the beginning of the performance, the acrobat seems to be in a world of his own. However, if you think about it, you will realise that he is talking to the audience through his art. There is an undeniable rapport between the acrobat and the audience, which is how he has them in thrall.

The acrobat flips; he spins, he flies, he leaps! The swings that he takes in quick succession are orchestrated to perfection, making your head spin. You excitedly attempt to keep track of his movements as he hooks his knees over a fly bar, reaches back and closes his grip on his fellow acrobat on the trapeze, who catches him easily. Then the catcher—the fellow who caught him—twists and throws the acrobat back to the fly bar in a move called 'return.' This is followed by a front and back somersault, a piggyback, and a passing leap. All these aerial tricks can make you feel quite dizzy! But the acrobat, not so much.

The acrobat is all there, in the moment, fully alive and completely absorbed. He just seems to be doing so many things at once and so effortlessly! You are amazed by his flexibility. You cannot help but marvel at his integration, strength and alignment. You are impressed by the control he has and the single-minded focus with which he performs on stage. Maybe the acrobat has left you in stunned silence, maybe he has left you envious. Now you have started to wonder, "How can I possibly be like an acrobat?"

Aren't You An Acrobat?

Mama will tell you right at the outset that you are entirely capable of accomplishing similar, even better, feats of acrobatics in your life. You have what it takes to get there; you only need to channel the inner acrobat in you. As mentioned earlier, the acrobat in the circus actually signifies you in your life. Though it may seem impossible, believe it when Mama says that you, too, can have the flexibility, the balance, the agility, the strength, and the focus of an acrobat. You can have all of that, but only if you commit yourself to developing these qualities in yourself.

As you watched the acrobat perform and, later, you processed the visual marvel that had unfolded before your eyes, several points might have struck you: the attention to detail, the quickness, the distinctive elegance, the eloquent expressions, and the meticulous choreography, all of which contributed towards crafting the dramatic spectacle of the acrobat's performance. You might be wondering just how much work went into perfecting the acrobat's performance. You might be questioning Mama's assertion that you, too, could emulate and hone all these qualities of the acrobat.

You will understand when Mama says to you that balance and agility come from a deep awareness of your body. You will read more on that later; for now, focus on drawing the right parallels between yourself and the acrobat. Let's first talk about the mental acrobatic skills that you know and exercise, or shall I say those that you possess but still don't exercise? It is true that some of those skills may be present in you already, however, they may be latent and you may not have utilized them yet. At this point, the importance of self-awareness must be reiterated to underline how vital it is if you want to realize your potential and live the life that you deserve.

As you face the different challenges life throws at you, do you not become adept at handling whatever comes your way? Do you not learn the art of landing on your feet in troubled times? Did you not develop your skill of maintaining or regaining your balance after you were dealt a particularly tricky curveball? Do you not practice swings, leaps, and somersaults like those of an acrobat as you navigate your way through life?

You perform so many acrobatic feats in life unwittingly

without realizing their significance. That accounts for the mental ability of the acrobat that you have within yourself, which you can develop as you grow older, provided you become self-aware and more accepting of yourself. Now, if you want to develop the physical attributes of an acrobat, you will need to know more about your body and taking better care of it than you presently do.

Your Body And Diet

It is important that you know your body if you want to enjoy a healthy existence. How do you think the acrobat is able to perform the gymnastics that are a part of his circus routine so well? How do you think the acrobat acquires the agility and nimbleness exhibited during his act? If you want Mama to put it in simple words for you, here is the answer; the acrobat is able to perform those demanding and dangerous acts only because he is physically fit. He fulfills the other requirements of focus and determination, yes, but more importantly, he is a robust and athletic person who has obviously spent time and energy in building up his physical state.

Your body is an exquisite machine. It breathes, walks, ands talks etc. It practically does everything for you. You go through the motions unconsciously every day without ever stopping to think about them. The importance of your body hits home only when you are sick and cannot function optimally as you do when you are in good health. Take lessons from the acrobat and realize how important it is to be aware of and take care of your physical health.

You consume food and drinks; the body uses what it needs and gets rid of what it does not. Take the time to notice how your body has grown over the years. Think of how tall you have grown, how your muscles have changed, and how your physique has developed after you hit puberty. As you do that, also make sure of the right food type for you. Which is the food that you like and which is healthy for your body? You should know which nutrients your body needs so that you can increase their intake. Also, you must be aware of the unhealthy food that you might be consuming and assess the negative impact it has on your health. It is crucial here that you exercise some self-discipline and revamp your dietary habit so that it is healthy and wholesome.

Now think of healthier foods that you can eat. For example, consider fish. Some people do not consume fish because they don't like its taste or smell. However, they should pause to think of the many health advantages of fish that they are missing. It is white meat and provides some essential nutrients that your body needs. Therefore, before you eliminate any food from your diet, do some quick research on its health benefits. Then you can try it; it is probable that you will develop a taste for it, and in the process, develop a more eclectic palate which would make you want to try new foods and have new culinary experiences!

As you mature and enter your twenties, you will be

able to acknowledge the nutritional requirements of your body and be more willing to improve your health. This usually isn't the case with younger people who eat without being concerned about the bad effects that junk food can have on their health. It is advisable that you evaluate your diet. Think about the things that you start to crave suddenly, like chocolate or coffee. Take it as a signal that your body is trying to send you. When you actually start to listen to your body instead of ignoring it as most people do, you will become a much healthier individual. You will get less sick and will be more physically fit.

The acrobat's skill—his precision and control—comes from having a healthy and fit body. So will yours. You need to pay attention to what you consume and weed out anything that may be hazardous to your system. Think of the particular nutrients that your body needs and take them in the right quantity. Excess of anything is bad for your health. The acrobats, you will see, come in all shapes and sizes. Yet, they are all capable of performing splendid physical feats due to their powerful muscle strength.

You can do the same. You too can build your physical stamina and develop strong muscles. All you need is strong willpower and determination to train your body, like an acrobat, and be as focused when it comes to fortifying your health. Then you can take long strides forward towards having an active and vigorous life.

The Right Information

Just as your body needs the right kind of food, so does your brain need the right kind of information to be sharper and keener. You need to exercise your intellectual muscles just as much as you need to exercise your physical ones. Though you will be inundated by information (after all, the modern world is marked by information overload), your job is to let the right kind of information in and leave the useless material out. You need to decide the kind of debates to participate in, for one thing. This applies to both, real-life debates and online discussions, and you know that the latter abound in this age, even more than the former.

Think about the people you engage with daily and the situations that you find yourself in on a routine basis. Do you get talking to people about things that are, in truth, meaningless to you? Are you dragged into arguments that do not concern you? Or do you put your foot down and avoid discussions that are of no benefit to you? The wisest option is to keep away from debates that drain you of energy and fill you with negativity. You have to learn when to get involved and when you should stay on the sidelines.

For this, you need to understand where your passions lie—what are the topics that truly interest you, what are the subjects that intellectually excite you and what are the current trends that you are concerned about? Yes, Mama asked you to engage with people when in the queue; however, do not waste time interacting with people who have little to offer by way of knowledge and wisdom. Also, understand that gossip will work like rust on the capabilities of your brain; it will distract you from the things that really matter. So, make it a point to remain focused on the important things.

It is not wise to talk for the sake of talking. Likewise, it is not advisable to read and be influenced by unverified or inflammatory information. The material you peruse will end up determining your beliefs, your thoughts and behaviour. So, filtering of information on the basis of its credibility and objectivity will serve you well, both in the long and short run.

This is what the acrobat does too. He knows what to focus on and what to ignore. If he gets distracted by all the information that surely surrounds him as much as it surrounds you, he'd never be able to perform the complex physical tricks that he does. Be like an acrobat then, and find out what you don't need to concentrate on; this is as, if not more, important as determining what to focus on in life.

The Right Choices

Do you know that as the acrobat performs difficult and tricky physical feats, he knows already that not everyone will applaud him for his work? He realizes that not everyone will appreciate his hard work, not everyone will support his actions and not everyone will understand his interests. The acrobat is conscious of this, and yet, he performs in front of large audiences as if none of that matters. That is accurate; it really does not matter how many people stand behind you and how many against. If you are true to your passion and your heart, the right kind of people will find their way into your life. This applies to friends, family, and others that you may encounter at different stages of your life.

The acrobat ignores the pain, both physical and mental. He persists and is consistent because he knows that the show must go on. The show, that is your life, must also go on, no matter what. Here, you will have to build your mental fortitude to bar negativity. To storm your way ahead in life despite discouragment, critical people pointing their fingers at you, is true courage. You must, however, make an effort to forge strong connections with the right kind of people. These are the people who applaud you when you are your best and who stand against you when you are not.

You must also maintain boundaries when it comes to your relationships with people. For example, if your friends say things which bother you or make you uncomfortable, then you need to let them know. Furthermore, as you grow in self-awareness, you must also ascertain what kind of people to surround yourself with and whom to filter out. You have to protect yourself from maliciousness. Remember, not all the burdens of the world are yours to carry.

The acrobat knows that self-care is important. He knows that his relationship with others is also important, but it always comes second. Consider this; the acrobat will mount the trapeze rope, execute his routine and at the moment that he is ready to jump to the next trapeze, he will let go of the first trapeze. Likewise, to get to the next trapeze you, too, must let go of the first one. For example, the first trapeze can be your school which you let go of to get to college. As you come to crossroads in life, as you will many times, you might have to make some tough decisions. You might have to decide to leave some family members or friends behind. But this is necessary for you if you want to move to the next phase, the next trapeze.

You are driven by the need to place your feet on solid ground and to maintain your balance. You will come across all sorts of people as you go along, just as the acrobat does. The acrobat knows his fellow artistes—he knows their strengths, their weaknesses, their fears, and their motivations. He knows that he is in competition with them at the same time, he is working with them. Everyone is interdependent; however, there comes a time when you have to make the decision to step to the next stage. Connections may be formed for a limited period of time; however, it is their quality rather than their duration that counts.

The Tightrope Called Life

Mama hopes that after reading this chapter, you were able to understand how the acrobat is a representation of yourself. The acrobat was presented to you so you could draw parallels between yourself and him and see the likeness that makes you as strong and agile as him. As you make this comparison and spend time understanding it, you will definitely grow in terms of self-awareness and self-confidence. You now also realize the importance of occupying the vantage point and making informed choices; this came, as a part of your experience as the circus audience. The acrobat's unfailing hard work, his unrelenting pursuit of his dreams, his drive to perform, come what may, are all intended to inspire you to do the same. After all, aren't you an acrobat too?

You know now that the acrobat perseveres through tough times and demanding physical training to demonstrate a dazzling show to you. The acrobat also taught you some crucial lessons about self-care; through him, you were able to see the importance of taking care of your own health, both physical and mental. He also imparted the wisdom of making the right choices—of taking in the right information and forming relationships with the right people. This is the way forward if you want your life to be fulfilling instead of disappointing.

Knowing yourself and then nurturing yourself precede knowing and caring for others. Only when you pay yourself the attention that you deserve will you be able to swing and slide on the tightrope called life with the ease of an acrobat. I know that it is not as easy and effortless as it seems; you need to put in a lot of hard work to make things flow smoothly in your life and to be content and happy. However, that is what Mama is here for. She will guide you along the way till you become as adept at living life as the acrobat is at maneuvering his way on the flying trapeze in the circus ring.

Chapter 4

TRAINED ANIMALS

The Animal Show

You have just watched the acrobat perform his unbelievable, awe-inspiring tricks. You had never seen anything quite like it. The acrobat's adroitness, balance, and flair, which enabled him to nail the acts, have left you speechless. At present, a short break has been introduced so the circus goers can get a breather from all the exhilarating acts. Though, you are still reeling from the excitement of the performance, you can't help but applaud the acrobat's body control and grip over his art, sharpened to perfection. You need the break to relax your mind, to slow down a little and anticipate the next act.

You walk around the circus, witnessing the sights yet again. Your mind at ease, you are ready to embrace the upcoming novel experiences about to follow. The trained animal show will begin in ten minutes. You observe the people around you. You see the lady with the confectionary, her smile sweeter than any of the sweetmeats she may have in her cart. You watch as people chatter and laugh, rubbing their hands in anticipation, waiting for the next thrilling performance.

As you stroll around the tents, a voice booms through the loudspeaker, "Attention, ladies and gentlemen! The show is about to resume! Tighten your seat belts for you are in for a wild ride. The animal show of our circus is all set to give you the time of your life. The animal show, dear guests, is about to begin!" With a flourish, the announcer declares open yet another circus treat. He then lays down some rules—not to use flashlights, to be quiet and considerate of other guests.

As you enter the circus tent once again, your brain goes into a quizzical mode. After all, till this point you have spent your time in the circus contemplating and drawing parallels from everything you have witnessed. Now, you are asking yourself what lessons are to be learnt from the next act. You are familiar with the animals that have been trained to perform at the circus today; elephants, big cats like lions and tigers, and horses, to name a few. The menagerie is ready and waiting—for your attention and applause. However, at this moment you can only think, "What are the parallels between me and the circus animals?"

The Animal Within

Once you start analyzing, you cannot stop. "What can the trained animals teach me about myself?" you wonder. "Which animal is present inside of me?" This leads you to other thoughts like, "Is the animal crouching within me trained?" Finally, you ask yourself, "How can I understand the animal outside and use it to better understand the animal within?" Mama is pleased that you have understood one crucial aspect of this animal show. The animals that you see before your eyes represent you, in a sense. They embody the instincts that lie within you, be they beneficial or harmful. Moreover, the circus animals are trained and tamed, but what about the animal that is within you? Is it also tamed and restrained so that it does no harm?

The first animal to be guided into the circus ring is a lion. Watching this dangerous and majestic animal so close, you are struck, yet again, by a sense of wonderment and awe.

You look at its blonde mane, its amber eyes and graceful sinews that bespeak brute strength, as it strides in. Its leisurely tread that seems to convey indifference, is a camouflage of its acute alertness. He carries himself with grace, befitting the king of the jungle, spiced with a hint of danger. You are transfixed and wonder, "What is similar between the lion and myself?" The realization slowly dawns on you.

There is a lion that resides within you, too. This lion

may be untamed, wild, and threatening; conversely, it may be disciplined, calm and protecting. What your own lion is like depends on what you have been feeding it and how you have been treating it. What is within you is powerful but can it be as affirmative and protective, if trained right, as a lion?

The lion inside of you is your ego. Did you ever think you were walking around with lion-power inside yourself that could make or break your life? In any case, what Mama wants is for you to understand how the lion within can control you. She wants you to learn the ways by which you can train and prepare it to enhance the experiences your life circus has to offer.

The Brute Force Of Your Ego

Your ego has the force of a lion. An untamed one, that is. It can control you and drive your life for you. Now, the decision is yours to make, in which direction will you let your ego lead you and to which destination? Before you get to the task of taming your ego, you need to learn all you can about this lion. The first thing that you must know is that your ego thinks it is the master, just like how the lion thinks that it is the master of the jungle. It believes that it has full rights to preside over your soul and your entire existence basically. If you think about it, you will realize that your ego actually governs not only your behavior, but also your thoughts and beliefs; about yourself and the world.

The lion that is your ego believes that it is always right. Conversely, it thinks that others are usually wrong. It is a beast that never sleeps. Every waking hour that you spend is administered by the quirks and whims of your ego. The ego always judges; it takes no break from that job. It looks for information outside of you and files it away to form judgments and pronounce verdicts on everything—from the people you encounter in life to the situations you might find yourself in. Your ego uses subjective conceptions to form its own standards of judgment, against which it compares everything.

You may question if that is fair; the answer, certainly, is that your ego, more often than not, is very discriminating in its assessment of things outside of itself. Truth be told, it is often unfair in its assessment of even yourself. It has a skewed sense of perception that ensures that the standards that it creates remain unbalanced and incorrect. It is for this reason that you need to take your ego to task. It is for this reason that you must learn how to control the wild force of your ego so that it does not force you into making choices and committing acts that you will regret in life. If left to its own devices, your ego will make an enemy out of others and will also alienate you from yourself. Surely, you don't want that to happen?

Taming The Lion

Confronting the brute force of your ego is a difficult but necessary task. If you don't take this bull by the horns, so to speak, then you will be led down paths you never wanted to take in life. You see, your ego functions on assumptions, biases and prejudices, as well as an inflated sense of self-importance; more than you would be inclined to think. Imagine your ego as a glass wall—one that is invisible but certainly there, preventing others from reaching you and trapping you within the confines of your own existence.

The real purpose of your ego is to protect you, and to act as a defense. However, Mama thinks that it often goes overboard. Instead of allowing you to grow and develop as a person, by which I mean making you open and receptive to new experiences and people that you meet at the circus, the ego makes you fall into a trap. Instead of acknowledging, accepting, and learning from people, it rebuffs them. It judges them and ascribes labels to them. So, instead of feeling connected with others, you are left feeling detached.

Your ego, instead of accepting others with their differences, starts to criticize and condemn them. You begin to view people who are different from you with suspicion, forgetting that this difference is what makes each human being unique. You become close-minded and end up being judgmental. You not only judge people's appearance and actions, but also their intentions. You see, Mama understands that your ego is a two-edged sword; the more it judges others, the more it also judges itself, meaning you. The first step towards taming your ego is to understand the way it functions. Once you understand its standard operating procedure, you can work towards addressing and redressing the wrongs that it is liable to commit.

You can determine if your ego is under your control or if you are under its control by a simple test. Analyze yourself the next time you encounter a stranger. You will find that you almost automatically assess their appearance—the kind of clothes they are wearing, their shoes, accessories, and so on. You will try to determine their social or financial status, and even their level of education, based on their appearance. However, therein lies the rub. What might happen is this. You may find that a person with messy hair, an unkempt appearance, and shabby shoes is actually highly educated and knowledgeable. On the other hand, someone dressed to the nines with Gucci accessories might turn out to be ill-informed, not as tolerant, and accepting as you would expect, based on their appearance.

This teaches you one basic lesson; appearances can be deceiving. Your ego (lion) has the habit of leaping to conclusions based more on preconceived notions than facts. The next time you find yourself following this pattern, Mama suggests you stop before your opinions become beliefs. Such beliefs are likely to be erroneous, based as they are on first impressions. You need to investigate beyond the surface and reach informed conclusions that are balanced and fair.

Freedom Of Choice

Mama wants you to understand one thing; every

person has the freedom to make their own choices. You see, in the course of the circus—when standing in the queue, or during the many shows you attend, you will meet all sorts of people. Some will be like you while others will not. Their tastes and interests, likes and dislikes, and backgrounds will be greatly divergent from your own. The lion of your ego may want to categorize these people into simplistic groups; it may want to swallow the complexities that each individual has in one big bite so that it does not have to go through the trouble of dealing with, understanding and accepting them.

In short, the ego, based on the existence of undeniable differences, will steer you away from people. In the first chapter, The Queue, Mama talked to you about the importance of forming connections with people. However, the lion of your ego will trap you in an unseen iron cage. Instead of helping you build a rapport with the people in the circus who, after all, are sharing the experience with you, it will separate you from them. As a result, you will start to criticize them and then pigeonhole people based on your circumscribed way of approaching life.

Mama has one very important rule that she wants everyone to learn; freedom of choice is important. People need to have the liberty to make the decisions that they feel are right for them without fear of censure and judgment, without feeling like criminals on trial. Wrong representations and flawed interpretations of people, their lives and their actions, should never get in the way of you respecting everybody's choice to be who they want to be.

Think of life as a huge table—wide, expansive, with more variety than you thought was possible. Now, just like yourself, people will come to eat at the table. They will see the foods that are there before them. Some will pick mashed potatoes, some will go for the choicest delicacy called caviar, some will opt for raw victuals such as sushi, while some will only drink water. Between the assortment that is there on the table of life, and the range of people that are there in the world, you are sure to come across some very eclectic combinations that may or may not make sense to you. However, Mama wants you to understand one thing; making sense of people is never as important as accepting people. With all their incomprehensible, difficult, or unsophisticated tastes which, when boiled down, are a matter of opinion, people still remain people. You must learn to accept them as they are.

Yet another essential point to understand is that people's choices and their actions are not reflections of who you are. Their standard will invariably be different than yours. The measure of quality for them is different from what it is for you. As a result, what you might perceive as perfect will be mediocre for them or vice versa. Remember that people have different stories, which you don't know, but which shape them to be who they are. Respectful acceptance is a must if you want to have good relationships with those around you.

You Are A Reflection

Though you may find it hard to grasp at this point, try to understand when Mama says that when you stop labelling others, you will automatically stop labelling yourself. You can verify that through your personal experience as well. Labelling others and labelling yourself are two sides of the same coin. They are codependent; they feed off each other and survive in this way. Once you start accepting people for who they are, you will start to accept yourself too.

You see, when you stop aggressively stereotyping and categorizing people, you will also stop comparing yourself to them. Have you ever seen children playing together in groups? They accept and embrace their peers, without a care as to how different they may be from each other. This openness is a result of a big heart. The lion that is your ego, will not feel cornered anymore. Once that happens, it will no longer feel the need to fight or react destructively. It will calm down and do its real job—that of spurring your growth—instead of holding you back in chains. Then your ego will resemble the lion of the circus—one who acts and performs rather than reacts unthinkingly, and even violently, to all that happens around him.

The poise, composure and self-possession of a trained lion, who knows its strengths and understands how to use them to his best advantage, can be yours, but only if you feed the lion i.e., your ego, the right diet. You will see that you are a reflection. What you see in others are actually qualities that are within you. It is your ego's trick to project your own failings and weaknesses on others rather than recognizing and correcting them within yourself. In the process of understanding and then taming the lion of your ego, you will go a long way in knowing who you are, too, and that's just a side benefit of being a part of the animal show.

Feed The Lion Well

You need to nourish the lion of your ego with the right inputs. So, you often feed your ego with harmful rather than beneficial things and this comes back to harm you in the future. This fodder for your lion ego can come in many forms. First, Mama will tackle the ubiquitous social media. This is an age of information overload. You will be bombarded with one message after another, that will undeniably cost you valuable time. Under such circumstances, you need to carefully moderate what your ego is exposed to. After all, its level of health is what counts the most. Sift the information, such that you absorb only what is positive and relevant to you.

Mama suggests that you do not follow the herd mentality. Your ego might want to go with the dominant opinion for it finds that easy to do; it might succumb to peer pressure, for it might have been trained to please others at the cost of its own contentment, or at the cost of what is right. For this reason, you must strengthen your ego to withstand opposition. Never allow your ego to absorb outside influences that will divest it of individuality and uniqueness. You must realize that you are one of a kind; to give in to external coercive forces that will break the lion's spirit is something that must be avoided.

Laziness is yet another virus that may prevent your ego from outgrowing its early life biases and prejudices. It would do that by thwarting new knowledge that would challenge its predetermined notions. It is for the sake of the right nourishment of your ego that you must learn something new every day.

Remember, you need to understand your own worth before you expect other people to do the same. Stop measuring yourself by the yardsticks that others have devised. You are not a sum of all that you own. You are more than the material things that you possess. You are also more than the sum total of all that you do. Your real self transcends the confines of the measurables in your life.

Most importantly, you are not what others think of you. You are your own person. So do not let partial, uninformed definitions that others have of you, restrict the way that you see yourself. You need to clear your own misconceptions so that you understand yourself better.

In the same manner, you must understand that no man is an island. You aren't separate from others. You are interconnected with others around you, though your ego might convince you otherwise.

Mama has stressed that the things you own don't define you. Likewise, you aren't defined by the things that you don't own. Your ego might blind you into believing such oversimplifications. It might compel you to constantly compare which will only make you judge yourself or others. Mama wants you to escape the limitations that the ego-lion tries to impose on you. She knows you can do it and so do you.

So be like a child—curious and eager to learn. This will not just sustain a healthy ego, but will also add value to your life. And isn't that the most important objective in this circus of life?

Lead By Example

"Look up, laugh loud, talk big, keep the color in your cheek and the fire in your eye, adorn your person, maintain your health, your beauty and your animal spirits."

- *William Hazlitt*

As the animal show winds up and you stroll along the circus grounds, certain realizations dawn on you. Mama can bet that through this journey, you will have grown tremendously. The epiphanies that you will have will lead you down a path of self-knowledge and self-awareness. You will learn some basic facts about your life and about yourself. You will see that during the course of this show, the biggest animal i.e., the lion of your ego, as well as the smaller ones, will have been trained and tamed. You will find yourself in much better control and with more self-assurance than when you started out on this circus journey.

You will understand your own worth as well as that of others. You will realise that it is wiser to remain quiet if you cannot compliment people as undue harsh criticism of others might come back to haunt you. Mama hopes that you will grasp the crux of this chapter, which is that you add value to things rather than the other way around. You must separate things from yourself because then and only then will you see yourself for who you are. This awakening can only be possible if you learn to tame the beast within yourself. Though it, your lion-ego, will try to wrest control back from you, in time you will become its true master. You are, after all, the only trainer who can lead the circus of your life in the right direction.

Chapter 5

THE DANCER

"We dance for laughter, we dance for tears, we dance for madness, we dance for fears, we dance for hopes, we dance for screams, we are the dancers, we create the dreams."

- Albert Einstein

The First Step

As soon as the animal show ends, you see the announcer heading up to the stage. He raises himself on his toes and twirls around before addressing the crowd, "The dancer cannot wait to greet you, folks!" He motions with his arm towards the backstage area, stirring excitement as people crane their necks to steal a look if they can, and then declares, "The dance of the circus is about to be underway. So spin and swirl—but in your seats! The dancers will give you the time of your life. Please welcome them with a round of applause!" Then, as if to provide a preview of the performance to follow—which people seem impatient to watch, judging by their animated clapping and head bobbing—he moonwalks to the exit, drawing another peal of approving laughter from the audience.

The lights dim, sending the venue into temporary darkness. After a short moment that only builds more anticipation, the spotlight is turned on, its glare on the stage, illuminating the center in a large circle of light.

A dancer emerges from behind the red curtains. He walks jauntily to the front of the stage, then picks up a stick and swings it around. As if on cue, two dancers, one from his right and the other from his left, emerge, swaying to the reverberation of the piano keys. The tinkle and jingle continue to rise, setting the mood. Your eyes widen in excitement and curiosity, as the dance show gets underway, pulling in all the circus goers like a magnet. Everyone, including yourself is under the spell of the dancers.

The Dancers

You watch as the circus dance gets underway. One by one, more dancers appear on the stage as a voice calls out in a singsong manner, "Ladies and gentlemen! Boys and girls! Step right up, step right up! You won't believe your eyes! Behind this curtain is something you haven't seen before. Join me for the most amazing show on earth!" This sends the crowd into a frenzy and they start to wave their arms from side to side, swaying in time to the music that only gets louder and livelier. The chorus in the song croons these words, lengthening them out for effect, "Do you want to be wildly entertained? Things aren't always as they are famed!" The curtain is drawn open all the way through, revealing the entire stage before your eyes.

You watch amazed as some dancers of the troupe appear walking on their hands. You view the unexpected sight. It's as if the world was turned upside down for your eyes only. You cannot help but break into an instinctive round of applause. There is so much to see that you cannot absorb everything at the exact moment that it happens. Later, you will recall the images and you will be able to glean life lessons from them, as you have done through the circus up to this point.

Right now, you watch as the dance show progresses, bedazzling you with its colors, movements, and sounds. As you watch the show, you feel as though you were up there on the stage, dancing with the immaculate dancers when, in fact, you are right there in your seat—unmoving yet moved!

You watch as the dancers form double lines with their backs to the audience. Then suddenly, one of the dancers is thrown up in the air, as if she were a weightless child. The dancer, for the brief moments that she remains suspended in midair, appears lissome and poised. Then she lands gracefully on the hands waiting to catch her. The entire team begins to dance now, completely immersed in their act. Their moves communicate joy. In that moment, they are alive, and so are you.

The beat of the song is matched perfectly by the dancers' very precise and sharp moves. They jump up together, with their hands extended to the roof as if they were reaching up to pluck out the stars. You want to do the same! Their energy radiates through you. It's as if an electric jolt of excitement courses through your body. Just like the dancers, you want to surrender to the moment, and dance in a carefree state of mind. You start tapping your foot in time with the beat as you watch the dancers move in synchronization with one another.

They dance in fluid movements, twirling around in a circle that widens as they move, mirroring the blossoming of a flower. Then, they fall to the ground and roll around before leaping up to their feet and repeating the initial dance steps. You feel as if the dancers and the entire audience has come full circle.

The music dies softly and the dancers break apart into two teams before exiting the stage. You have still not processed the story that their dance narrated. You watched them move, keeping time with the music, and the beat of your heart. You saw them leap, turn, twist, and fall, only to rise again, gracefully, like swans. All through the dance performance, the dancers' fluid movements reminded you of flowing water. You were awed by their grace, poise, and movements which embodied a story, comprehended and interpreted differently by each person in the audience. In a sense, the dance was a secret code for every member of the audience.

The performance is over, but, for you, the story has just begun. Mama says this, because she knows that at the end of this dance show, you will follow Mama's guidelines and spend some time in introspection. You will try to identify the congruence between the dance and your own life. You will start to understand the underlying similarities and you will be able to comprehend how the dance of the circus is analogous to your life. You will see how the dancers are a representation of your individual self. You will begin to accept how you, too, are a dancer—one who is always engaged in an invisible but undeniable dance of life.

The Hidden Language

As you process the dance show in your mind, you will realise that dance is a language. Isn't this why you understood what the movements of the dancers meant and what the dancers were trying to communicate to the audience through their eloquent expressions? And that you could comprehend with ease, the hidden language of their dance throughout the performance.

Now, Mama urges you to repeat the exercise of drawing parallels between your inner self and the dancers at the circus, who effortlessly built a rapport with the audience in the short time they were on stage. Inside, each of us is a dancer who moves to the indiscernible music of their life. The tone and mood of the music changes as your inner landscape and external circumstances shift. As the music changes, so will your dance. Without being aware of it, you have been dancing all the dances that life has demanded of you all along.

Every dance needs completion. This is necessary if you want the feelings that led to the dance— such as happiness, fear, or even boredom—to find expression. Your dance is an affirmation, as well as a celebration of your life. Every human being's dance is individual to them. Likewise, all dances that you dance in life are different from each other. Your dances depend on the emotional song of your life. Moreover, it depends not just on yourself, but also on those around you. You are a dancer who stands alone, at the same time, you are a part of the team of dancers that collectively form humanity. Mama believes that understanding, accepting and appreciating your role in both the capacities is vital to living a meaningful life.

First of all, it is important that you identify the dance that you are engaged in currently. It is similar to reviewing the queue that you occupy. Once you reach a conclusion as to the type of dance you are performing, you will be better able to understand the nuances of your own complex internal life. You will realize that there are many dances that you have danced in life. More importantly, that often you have danced more than one dance at the same time. The dance that you perform all depends on the way you feel at that time.

For example, you will dance the dance of happiness when you are elated, your feelings expressing your inner state. Think of little children who spontaneously and unguardedly break into dance when they feel like it. In their case, dance is an artless, instinctive expression of their inner condition. There is no purer expression of joy than a child's dance. Mama advises you to learn from a child's dance and view it as a way to heal your soul and make yourself feel better. Dance can be an expression of joy, but can also induce joy in you when you feel down and out.

Then there is also the dance of boredom. Let's call it the bear dance. When you have everything at your fingertips—books to read, movies to watch, games to play and people to talk to, yet feel disenchanted and uninterested, you are dancing the bear dance. This dance exemplifies the tediousness of daily routine, the listlessness and weariness that might envelop you. The bear dance can teach you to change your inner state. Once you recognize the bear dance that you have been dancing, you can work towards changing the dance pattern. You can modify your thoughts, which will then alter your dance. Shifting your perspective, then, can transform your bear dance to, maybe, the dance of happiness.

You might also discover your own dance of pain. This dance obeys a different melody. It is a waltz with yourself. You clasp your arms around your own body and hold yourself close, so that the whole world is shut out. Then you dance to the rhythm of your own anguish. You glide and swirl to the song of your sorrow. You rise and fall on the mirrored dance floor that endlessly reflects your lonely image. Once you recognize that you have been dancing this waltz, you might be propelled to change your inner state. You might alter the tune of pain to one of, perhaps, contentment. As you shift the tune, the dance you have been dancing will also change.

You should consciously ensure that the lyrics of the song you dance to be joyful and happy. Mama says this because the lyrics can make your spirits soar or plummet. So choose the wordings wisely. The lyrics should neither be derogatory nor hurtful. If you want to feel at peace, then the language of your songs should be full of love. It should embrace everyone regardless of differences. Remember, the lyrics express your inner state. So exude only positive vibes, for what you send out will always make its way back to you.

Mama wants you to keep in mind that you can always select the rhythm that you dance to. Just as you saw the dancers in the circus transition from one dance step to another, you too can shift the dance of your life. You have already learned the importance of balance and agility from the acrobat. Now you can apply the same to your dance. Remember, mere possession of knowledge is not enough. You must put that knowledge into practice to maximize its benefits.

Dancing Solo

There is something intrinsically unique about you—something within you, of which no copy exists. This thing that you cannot quite put a name to, always manifests in the dance of your life. This is also what makes your dance one of a kind. No one can imitate the magnificence of the dance that is born out of your individuality and creativity. So when you dance solo, as Mama talked about earlier when she said that you stand alone as a dancer, you will uncover your own exceptional qualities that make you who you are and set you apart from the rest of the world.

You must have become aware of the individual dancing prowess of the circus dancers as they danced before you on stage. For you, perhaps, one or two out of the entire group may have stood out. Other audience members may have settled on other dancers as their favorites. The point is that even though the dance troupe may have performed together, their individuality shone through. This was something they could not repress nor did it go unnoticed by the audience. Each dancer's specific talent, hard work, and singular determination to give their best during the performance, would inadvertently be communicated to the viewers.

Likewise, you are unique. The dance that you perform in life must reflect your true personality, of which no replica exists in the world. Mama will caution that this might require you to relinquish the use of branded objects, which stamp you with their own mark and strip you of every strand of originality. Your sense of uniqueness is overridden by someone else's idea of who you should be. Mama urges you to maintain your individuality. Do not allow others to influence you. Perform your own dance as others watch, mesmerized by your self-awareness and self-assurance.

A Sea Of Movement

As you dance through your life, you will realize that though you are your own person, you are also part of a team. Now, this team may be the people who you live close to, such as your family, friends, colleagues, or neighbors or, on close scrutiny, you may find that you belong to the dancers' team called humanity. This is what Mama alluded to earlier. Once you take a sweeping glance at your life and the world, you will realise how interconnected your life is to those around you, and to the entire human race. You are an integral part of a sea of movement, comprising every human being you have come across and interacted with during your life.

Yes, you are an individual with your own specific set of strengths and weaknesses; however, as you comprehend and appreciate how enmeshed you are with others, you will appreciate the subtle advantages of being a part of this cascading sea. You will see that dancing with others has its own benefits unmatched by dancing alone. You will acquire the skills and learn how to become a dexterous dancer, the most important being, never to step on others' toes. Dancing with others will teach you how not to dance toe-to-toe to avoid hurting yourself or others during the dance of life.

For example, as a team member, you will notice the small flaws in your dancing technique—the few missteps, the one movement you made missing the beat. All of this can be covered quite effortlessly by the people whom you are dancing with. Their strengths will mask your weaknesses. Your team will complement your skills, they will camouflage your shortcomings, and enhance your strengths. When in a team, you work hand in hand with others to present the best dance performance you can. This will teach you the significance of collaborative work and of finding your place in a a sea of individuals who may be equally or more talented than you. In short, you will be more in tune with others as well as yourself.

Interacting with others, clashing with them, getting along with them and working your way through the hiccups that are a part of any teamwork, will contribute immensely towards your growth. You will learn not only about the dance pattern of others, but also your own. You will thus find that embracing the sea of movement not only helps you to understand others better, but also yourself.

The Winner Waltz

"Dancers are made, not born."
- Mikhail Baryshnikov

By now, you must have realized that life made you a dancer who can twist, turn, glide, and leap with the grace and the fluidity of a circus dancer. Not only do you dance on your own as you progress through life, but you also dance with those you come into contact with. The invisible yet palpable dance that you engage in, on your own and with others, has made you an expert.

As you process all this information and apply it in your life, Mama hopes you understand that this world is a ballroom in which you have to take your rightful place. You should not sit around waiting for others to cheer you on or pull you up to become a part of the dance of humanity. This prerogative is all yours. You have to actively engage in the dance of life. You must remember that your space is reserved on that dance floor. All you need is to fall in step.

So, you have learned how the dancers dance; you understand their coded language, and the significance of dancing solo and in a team. Mama wants you to learn one more important lesson here; to dance the winner waltz under any circumstance. This is, first of all, a call for you to celebrate instantly your own joys and successes. You must surrender the habit of waiting around for others to join in and drive your celebratory dance. The happiness is yours and thus, its expression must also be yours. The positive after-effects of immediate celebration will also be immediate.

Lastly, you must carefully watch those around you

and decide whether or not you want to join in their dance routine. Remember to follow your natural instincts and intuition. The point of the dance is not to force you into a mold devised by others, but to enable you to realize your latent dancing potential. Dancing the winner dance is all about dancing to the tune of your own heart. It is a celebration of your life, despite its failures and setbacks. Mama wants you to take the failures in your stride because they teach you essential lessons regarding life. So kick off your shoes, feel the beat and vibration of Mother Earth, and dance to the music. Dance through rain and through sunshine. Do that till every cell in your body joins in the celebration.

Chapter 6

THE TRAPEZE

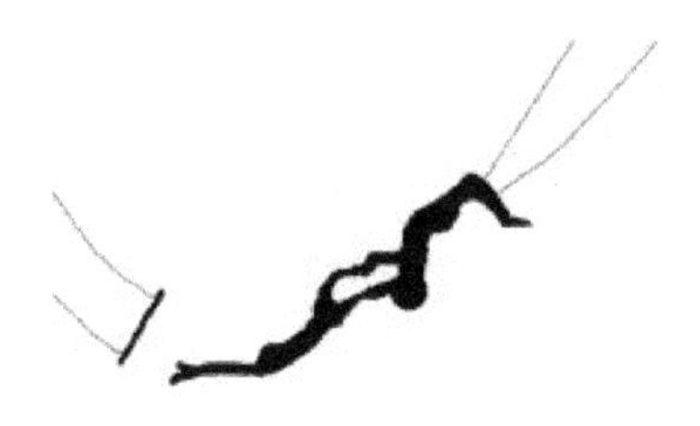

"He'd fly through the air with the greatest of ease. That daring young man on the flying trapeze."

- Popular Song

In The Air

The circus dance has ended. Now, you are waiting for the next show to start. Seated in your chair, you look around. The people who were in the circus queue with you have watched the shows that you have watched. Till now, they have shared the circus journey with you. Though you have all apparently been through the same trip, you know that everyone will have taken away different lessons. What you learn so often depends on what you are willing to learn. Opening the mind's eye to the lessons that can be learned from the circus is no mean feat. However, Mama believes that you have what it takes to join the dots, make the right connections, before the quirks of the circus begin to make sense to you.

The circus dancers' act taught you not only about your role as an individual, but also as an interconnected, interdependent component of the team called humanity. However, the external journey is as important as the journey within. You need to look inward just as much as you need to look outward so that you can have a balanced perspective in your life. Meanwhile, in the circus, the trapeze show is about to begin. The announcer traipses onto the stage, singing the old song, "He'd fly through the air with the greatest of ease…a daring young man on the flying trapeze…his movements were graceful, everyone he could please…and my love he has stolen away!"

The crowd seems to know the song; they start singing along with him and, soon, the circus tent transforms into a place of cheerfulness, where everyone sings in unison, often discordant, but with harmony in their hearts. As the song comes to an end, the announcer gives a deep, dramatic bow and with some fanfare, announces the beginning of the next show, "Without further ado, ladies and gentlemen, I proclaim the next show open. It is time to clap your hands for the trapeze artists! Their performance will leave you speechless!" With that, he quickly slides off the stage, allowing the new show to grip the audience. They watch on with anticipation as a familiar excitement envelops them.

Swaying Slow

One by one, the trapeze artists enter the ring. Soon, the stage is occupied by a group of trapeze artists, ready to perform for their enthralled audience. Meanwhile, the stage, too, has been transformed for the act. Now you can see bars and ropes hanging from the ceiling. These are props essential to the performance. The show begins and you witness a spectacular display of strength, balance, agility, precision, and control. One by the one, the artists take their places, and start swinging on the ropes and bars. Captivated by their smooth but complex moves, you can't help but notice how well their movements are synchronized with each other.

First, you watch the swinging trapeze where the artist grabs the bars and swings backward and forward, building momentum with each cycle. His movements are precisely timed. He hangs with his hands clutching the bar and then does a sudden flip, making your heart flip in return. He catches the bar with his ankles, then bracing his hands between the rope and the bar, swings to the next one. You admire the strength and grace with which he finishes his task.

Next up are the artists on the flying trapeze. The performer, called a 'flyer,' captures the bar between his hands and jumps off an elevated stage. You watch with your heart in your throat as the performer swings back on to the stage and takes yet another swing forward. He aims for the second swing at the far end and as he lunges forward to grab that bar, he does a somersault in the air, catching people by surprise. He propels himself to the next bar, where another performer awaits to catch him; he is the designated 'catcher' who is hanging by his knees on another trapeze. He catches the first performer gracefully and the two begin an intricate dance. They perform in tandem with each other, their movements perfectly coordinated, and in harmony.

You are amazed by the first performer's implicit trust on the second to catch him in time. You are impressed by the courage it must take for the performers to take successive leaps at the risk of not being able to land safely. Yet they perform with immense courage and dedication, without compromising on the flair and style required. You see how all the performers are trained to bear each other's weight while displaying strength, grace, and sprightliness to ensure a perfect act. You witness the artists spin and swivel in the air, perfectly calm as they embrace the moment of uncertainty; the time between the two bars. You envy their courage, as they complete the perilous feat with precision.

Their costumes are brightly colored, but their talents shine more vividly. Mama believes that by now, you are able to look beyond the external appearance of things to what lies beneath the surface. She hopes that you can see that his performance is a culmination of days of hard work. It was through their arduous efforts that the artists were able to put up a show worthy of the loudest applause. The toil of the trapeze artists is evident once you look past the glitz and witness the reality behind the curtains. That's when you will begin to see how your life, and the way you live, resembles that of the trapeze artists.

Swinging Along Life

Once you start viewing the trapeze artists' performance from a different perspective, you will be able to draw some very insightful parallels between yourself and them. To the ordinary eye, a trapeze may appear to be just an apparatus made up of short horizontal bars, hung by ropes and metal straps, on which artists hang and swing back and forth. However, to you, the trapeze act seems like an ocean from which you can draw countless pearls of life-transforming wisdom. In retrospect, you will realize that this was the main point of the circus journey. Mama is happy that you have learned to find meaning beneath the glitter that often escapes others.

Now, you see life as a trapeze act where you have to constantly transition from one state to another, much like the queues Mama discussed with you earlier. You have to keep changing your queues in life to facilitate growth and improvement. This is exactly how the trapeze of life works. It demands that you swing from bar to bar and from rope to rope without pausing or giving up. This, requires strength of the mind and generosity of the spirit, which would enable you to endure the transitions in life, often demanding and painful. But Mama knows that you have what it takes to meet life's demands head-on.

You will see that the trapeze act of life never lets you remain stationary for too long. If it were up to you, you might have found it easier to get to one place (comparable to one trapeze bar) and remain there because that would be comfortable and easy. Think of life's trapeze as the unseen force or catalyst that keeps driving you towards growth and improvement. You see, to move ahead you have to let go of the older things that you were holding on to. There is always a bar in front of you, which you must reach for, if you want to stride forward in life. However, to get to it, you have to let go of the bar you are currently grasping for dear life.

Do you remember when, as a child, you went to the park with your parents and played on the monkey bars? You clutched one bar, then the next, and thus got from one end of the swing to the other. Recall how proud you felt when you finished that short journey successfully. Sometimes, you may have slipped between the two bars; then, skinning your knees, you might have shed tears because of the pain of the fall. As you painstakingly pushed yourself across those bars, you must have felt the burning sensation in your strained muscles. However, all that pain was worth it, was it not, when you were able to finish what you had started?

Likewise, in life you have to take some steps forward, just like the trapeze artist, and you yourself did as a child. To be alive means to be dynamic. It means to undertake the task of transition from one phase to another. However, this may be painful, but the pain itself acts as an indicator of internal growth; of the evolution in your character. Ultimately, you must understand that inertia will only hold you back. To make the best of what life has to offer, you need to embrace change, grasp and swing across the trapezes that spring your way.

Between The Bars

As you leap from trapeze to trapeze in life, you will realize that those few moments where you are suspended between the two bars are a representation of the uncertainty that you face in life. You just watched the trapeze artists swing from one bar to another; you saw how, for an interminable instance, they were suspended in midair. You feared the many possible ways that instant of suspension could go. Now, people might be daunted by those few moments of uncertainty, enough to give up the entire task of getting to the next bar. However, Mama would like you to ask yourself, would that be the right thing to do? Should fear and anxiety about all that could go wrong prevent you from taking those steps forward?

Mama understands the fear that comes with uncertainty. She knows that when you are in between two bars, you are anxious and fearful about the possibility of falling from a height and its life-threatening consequences. However, to let true evolution happen, you have to step out of your comfort zone. That moment between the bars when you are swinging—when you have let go of one bar but haven't yet grabbed another—you might feel as if you are suspended in a void that might swallow you up. However, Mama asks you to pause and reflect; aren't you the most alive in those few moments? Aren't you at your very best in that fraction of time when your attention is the sharpest and your focus the keenest, even though your heart seems in your throat?

You must release your grip on the first bar—though it is one that you have become familiar with—to get to another strange bar. This may fill you with terror because the unknown can be terrifying. You are hurtling yourself forward and for the time being, you are dangling over a wide space that feels like a deep chasm. However, you have to take the leap of faith to get to the next bar of life. Mama will share a simple trick: just tell yourself that there is no alternate way. There is just this one road, this one route.

Consequently, you must let go of the older, familiar bar and grab the new, strange one. Once you do that, you will soar over your own fears. In that moment when you are poised between two bars—confused, disoriented, and scared—you will learn to embrace your own humanness. It is all right to be afraid. It is only human to feel that way. However, take this opportunity and learn to overcome those feelings.

This space between the bars where you feel pushed out of your comfort zone can be a rich source of self-awareness, wisdom and growth. Mama is confident that you will find that on your own as you move from bar to bar on the trapeze act called life. You will learn that you, too, are entirely capable of flying through the air with the grace and poise of a circus trapeze performer.

Tapered Targets

Mama knows you are worried about where you will land as you move from one bar to the next. Now, your focus is not on the state of transition but on the place where you will arrive once you let go of the older bar. As you take the leap, however, you will realize the ocean of strength, determination, and courage within you. After all, if you were not equipped with these qualities, you would not have made it so far in this journey through the circus. The fear of transformation has now given way to another fear: the fear of what your dream or target actually looks like. What is it that you are going towards? What is it that you are leaving behind to get to your new goal, your new destination? Have you ever paused to analyze why you have set yourself the targets that you have?

Mama has a theory about your targets and dreams that she would like to share with you: your material goals are merely a short-term manifestation of your long-term, deeper targets. For example, a fancy car or a big beautiful home may not be your dream itself, but a symptom of your underlying dream to be financially and socially strong. Once you realise this, you must ask yourself if this dream that you think you have; whose is it in the first place? Is this dream yours or did someone else shape it for you? And what makes you accept their dream, goal, and target for you? Is it right to accept another's idea as your own dream, even though it may have little to do with who you really are?

Mama wants you to examine the dreams that you think are your own. Consider their motivation and source and ascertain whether or not they truly are your dreams. Then take steps accordingly. Often, society tries to box people in. When children are sent to school, they are made to conform to the older, traditional methods of being. According to society, these methods instill similar dreams in everyone, ones that are tried and tested, and hence, safe. However, this restricts children from dreaming new dreams for themselves.

The problem is systemic, but everyone must put in an effort to bring about change. Mama knows how these older ways of living can only bestow old and outdated dreams on the young dreamers. This is regressive and affects the evolution of the entire human race. So it is important to free yourself from the shackles of outdated models of dreams. Decide your own targets and work towards them. This is the only way that you can be true to yourself and bring a positive change in the world at the same time.

Take The Leap To Your Dream

Dream your own dreams. Mama only wants to encourage you to pursue your dreams as your dreams are important. Though there may be cultural constraints on you, you must still fearlessly follow your heart. Keep refreshing and renewing your dreams to keep pace with the times that you live in. Dream big, but also dream smart. If there is one way that you can make your life remarkable, it is by following your heart. Though this may, for a while, give you the feeling that you are no longer in control, but being controlled and guided by your dream allows the change to take place because Mama knows the end result will be rewarding.

Do not allow others to hijack your dreams. Things around us are changing and evolving at a very rapid pace. So when you dream, be progressive and innovative. Do not allow yourself to be boxed into stereotypes. Equip yourself with the information and knowledge to make things happen. Learn everything that will enable you to achieve your dream. And if a dream does not materialize exactly the way you wanted, do not be disheartened. Take it as a necessary life lesson for there are many more trapezes that you can hold on to and let go of as you progress through life.

I quote an anonymous person, "We cannot discover new oceans unless we have the courage to lose sight of the shore."

So, take a deep breath and leap with the firm belief that you will make it.

Up Above The World So High

"For the trapeze artist to grab the next bar, she has to let go of the last one."

- Gail Blanke

As you go from trapeze to trapeze in life, you will simultaneously go through the journey of self-enlightenment and self-improvement. You watched the trapeze artists put on a spectacular performance. You witnessed them swing from bar to bar, exhibiting dexterity, strength and agility; at the same time, you admired their mental skills of embracing fear and uncertainty to take the next step forward. Mama was along with you as you learned how expansive the moments of suspension can be and how enriching life lessons can be, if only you are willing to see the truth and accept it.

Mama also taught you how to make productive use of the time between bars to enable the growth of your character and attitude towards life's challenges. At the same time, Mama warned you against pursuing dreams that are mere copies of others' ideas, as this could keep you from discovering your true potential.

As the trapeze act ends, Mama reiterates; flying from one bar to another in life will need daring and determination. She believes you have those two qualities within you to make the jump successfully.

This moment is one bar that is preparing you for the next bar. So just shift your perspective and draw on the courage that is within you. The next bar of the trapeze called life is full of possibilities that will transform your existence.

Chapter 7

COTTON CANDY

"Life is not made just of miracles,
roses and cotton candy."
- Anonymous

The Carnival Taste

As you wander across the circus grounds in the lull between the shows, you are attracted to other enticements around. By this time, everything in the circus has started to seem more profound and meaningful to you. Simply stated, you have learned that there is more to the circus than meets the eye. However, Mama knows that now you can see the extraordinary in the seemingly ordinary things. So, as you walk through the crowds, you let your eye wander over the other marvels that the circus has on display. In the surging wave of people who are busy discovering the victual wonders, your eyes are caught by color floating on air; cotton candy.

Made almost entirely of sugar, cotton candy looks like a small cumulonimbus cloud caught on a stick. The image of cotton candy may even make you imagine an arm stealthily reaching up to the sky, quickly grabbing handfuls of swirling clouds and cleverly heaping them up on a thin stick to give you a fluffy, cottony treat. Or it might resemble the fur on little sheep. Your mind might recall the Cotton Candy Sheep of the children's book Charlie and the Chocolate Factory. In its made-up world, special sheep with cotton candy fur were reared and later sheared by the Oompa Loompas, collecting this fur as a choice confection. It looked magical, didn't it? It does seem fitting that the story conjured a fanciful treat as whimsical as cotton candy.

Now, cotton candy is synonymous with the circus. Cotton candy is and has been staple circus fare for a long time now. In fact, it seems to be as crucial to the circus as the joker himself. So this is what catches your eye out of all the other foodstuff on display. You amble towards the cotton candy stand, dwelling on the similarities that you are now certain exist. You are now programmed to glean invaluable lessons from even the most inconsequential aspects of the circus.

Mama has faith that the lessons you will learn from the cotton candy will illuminate yet another aspect of your existence and present a new way of looking at things.

A Sweet Bite

The cotton candy stand is a bright pink contrast to the pastel clouds of sugar it spins for the circus goers. Its neon color screams for attention and people obediently flock towards it. The cart contains a big bowl within which the vendor concocts the wispy fluffy treat. Cotton candy is made of melted sugar which, by the use of centrifugal force, spins through tiny holes to produce woolly confectionary. As you draw close to the stall, you are able to see for yourself the precise and elaborate process undertaken by the vendor to whip up this delectable candy for the circus goers.

As you watch, you realize that something as seemingly uncomplicated as cotton candy, actually demands a measure of dexterity. After all, the candy, though light and foamy, must not collapse. It should not be too gauzy or too stiff. So you are keenly trying to understand the hard work and skill which goes into its execution.

The vendor takes a small container and adds some sugar, syrup and water. He then stirs the mixture vigorously. The sugar mixture is now a pink color. He adds a small spoonful of it to the machine's spinning bowl. Brandishing a narrow stick, the vendor twirls it around the machine as if it were a magic wand. You watch as thin clouds of cotton candy gather around and cling to the stick as the vendor continues to give it turn after giddy turn. Soon, a generous puffy mass is gathered around the stick, which is cotton candy for you. It looks partly like a cloud, and partly like the hair of an old granny.

You buy the cotton candy from the vendor, eager to taste it. As you dig into the promising cloud, you are forced to close your eyes to better appreciate the flavour. The spun sweetness melts in your mouth, and your taste buds are bombarded with sugar. You admit to yourself that feeling the sweetness comes not only from the candy but from the circus experience itself. To you, the taste of the circus is associated with the taste of cotton candy. From now on, the taste of cotton candy will evoke the memory of this circus experience. Mama says this because she knows how strong the bonds of association are in the memory of human beings.

As you finish your cotton candy, you strike up a conversation with the vendor. You are only applying what you have learned so far in the circus; you have understood that interacting with the people who are in the same queue as yours, even for a short time, makes for enriching encounters. The vendor relates the tale of the invention of the cotton candy machine to you. You find it utterly interesting and ironical that it was, in fact, a dentist called Dr. Morrison who co-created this "electric candy machine" with the confectioner, John Wharton. It proved to be quite a lucrative venture for them back in the late 19th century. You also learn that cotton candy was first christened "fairy floss," probably a more suitable name for it. Furthermore, you discover that several centuries ago, cotton candy was a delicacy that only royalty could afford.

As you trace the development of cotton candy through the years, you cannot help but ruminate over the trajectory of its evolution as a confectionary item. It fascinates you how cotton candy changed from a money-spinning product that catered only to the aristocrac,y to one that is readily available to the masses today. You wonder what spurred that progress and soon, your brain does the math and credits the ingenuity of the human mind for this turnaround.

You start thinking of the other boundless ways that the human mind has revolutionized life and continues to do so. You are awed, but also inspired.

The Inquisitive Eye

To your inquisitive eye, the swirls of cotton candy seem to carry messages meant only for you. You begin to decipher the code encrypted in the whirls of cotton candy. The sugar represents knowledge, and the process of its creation symbolizes the creative spirit of human beings. As you observe the candy, you become increasingly aware of the way you function. You observe things, listen to people talk about them, and then arrive at a conclusion. The more you notice things around you, the more you learn about yourself.

So how does the sugar of the cotton candy symbolize knowledge in the circle of life? The answer is quite simple, and Mama thinks you already know it. Sugar works to sweeten all things that it is added to, doesn't it? Such is the case with knowledge. If you add knowledge and wisdom to anything in life, like your educational career or your professional life, or even to your day-to-day conversations, you will see them transform from the mundane to the exceptional. Variety may be the spice of life, but knowledge is certainly its sugar. And we all need a bit of sweetness in our lives. After all, that is what makes it worth living.

So the sugar of knowledge enhances the good things in life. It directly relates to the intellect of human beings, their creative outlook, and pioneering attitude towards life and living. Sugar is indispensable if we want life to taste good and valuable, much like knowledge. Especially in the circus of life, where everyone needs a sweet bite or two to have a great time. You can confirm this as you watch the people around you. They are standing in line at the cotton candy stand, just like you did only a while ago, which shows that people are willing to wait for their happy dose of sugar.

As you continue to look around, Mama must stress the importance of observation. Everything you have learned so far in this circus of life has originated from your powers of observation. Just think about it for a moment. If you had not observed the people in queue, you would never have compared yourself to them and been moved to determine your own queue in life. If you had not noticed the joker, the acrobat, the animals and other circus attractions, you would never have sought the underlying meaning behind each of the acts. This is why Mama believes that knowledge of any kind begins with observation.

Moreover, your brain processes information based on what it perceives through the senses. The power of observation is the sense that people rely on most to grasp their surroundings. If honed, this power can help you notice things that are hidden in plain sight (things that others around you are unable to notice). Mama believes that the more you look outwards, the better you can look inwards as well. This only means that the more clearly you notice the outer world, the more you will realize that it is but a reflection or projection of your inner landscape.

Mama believes that the more you look at the world, the more you will become aware of the things that need to be changed and the more you will be pushed to your intellectual limits to come up with the best solutions. So what begins as an instance of strong observation will end in practical problem-solving endeavors, which will benefit not just you, but those around you. This is true of the greatest innovations and discoveries by man.

Take Isaac Newton for instance. Legend has it that as he rested on the grounds of a farm, he saw an apple fall from the tree to the ground. Now, this sight was probably observed by many before him. However, real power of observation means that what you see registers on a deeper level, as it did with Newton.

The genius that he was, he made the right connection. He thought of the forces of nature, and concluded that the reason why everything gravitates toward the ground is because a force acts on all things, pulling them down to the earth. The discovery of the force of gravity (which was around since life began on earth) was only possible because Newton observed, in the truest sense of the word, and made the right connections.

This brings us to yet another finding: observation can lead to innovative, original solutions. It is in the spirit of human beings to look for solutions once they encounter a problem. Now, if you lead an anesthetized existence with your power of observation remaining dormant, you would never come across any problems. You will be complacent, thinking all is well, and that there is no need for change. However, someone with a keen eye would notice the many things around that could be fixed or improved. They would strive for advancement and be driven to find creative solutions. This is how achievers are born.

Solving Problems

Problem solving is an invaluable skill in the world today. There are many concerns that need to be confronted and fixed. However, before you think of solutions and problems in vague terms, Mama would like to present you with an example that illustrates the process of finding solutions. This example is of a man who learns to pay attention. Once he does that, he sees a problem that needs resolving, and gets down to the task. This is a man who is a regular bus commuter. He travels by bus, but from his window, he notices many of his fellow citizens commuting by renting bicycles. Their commute, however, is interrupted every time it rains. He sees the problem and wants to make things better.

So he thinks of possible ways to resolve the problem. Soon, he stumbles on an idea. He proposes that a low-cost shelter for the bicycle rental shop be built and an affordable canopy for the bicycle commuters be developed. This would allow the rental business to run and the cyclists to shuttle back and forth even on rainy days. Armed with this, he approaches the relevant people and they implement his proposal. His idea ultimately benefits the entire community. Do you see how it started? Just through observation. The bus commuter noticed the things that his fellow passengers let pass by. Therefore, Mama believes that the more you notice and pay attention, the more difference you can make to the world.

Solutions have to be creative to be effective. The creative process of human beings is propelled by observation as well as the needs and requirements of the environment. For observation is what motivates humans to correct the wrongs they see with inventive, amazing solutions. Moreover, solutions are driven by the environment in which the problem arises. This means that two similar or even the same problems can have different solutions, depending upon the context in which they are situated. Every setting is different; what may be applicable to one problem may not work in the same, successful manner in other circumstances. Solutions, then, need to stem from the context of the problem. In other words, solutions need to be adapted to the needs of the situation.

The biggest motivator for human beings to find solutions to problems is the human spirit. Why did the commuter come up with his plan? Not because he wanted to make money, but because he wanted the life of other commuters to be easy. So let that be your inspiration. Do not let mercenary motives drive you. If your inspiration stems from your position as a human being, then your solutions will also be entirely human in character, attempting to serve the needs of fellow beings.

The Call Of Creativity

Though poets have called imagination a bird free to take flight wherever it wants, reality often proves to be too harsh, so much so that it chains even the bird of creativity and imagination. These two, however, are the necessary ingredients of any recipe for human progress and evolution. If your imagination is bound by the restrictions or limits of family or culture, Mama suggests that you respectfully break free to explore the vast horizons of your own imagination. Human beings are born with the innate capacity to innovate and create. So you must not let artificial boundaries circumscribe your life. Remember, you came to the circus not only to learn but to make a difference.

There are always several ways to ensure that your creative spirit remains free to fly. You have ideas and theories, just like the great thinkers before you did. What you can do to ensure that your ideas are one day acknowledged is to note them down yourself. What Mama means to say is, you must take a notebook and pen and note down your ideas daily. You are naturally inquisitive. Now, you have started to notice things. You have started looking beyond the surface and to really see things as they are. Logically then, your brain will become a hothouse of thoughts, ideas, philosophies and theories. You need to remember them in order to refine them at a later time.

So make it a habit to note things down so you can work on them in the future—in case you do not have the time to reflect on them at present. Mama advises you to use even your limitations as advantages. For example, others might perceive your culture or your age or your family as impediments. However, if you change your perspective, you will be able to turn those limitations on their head. They will then become sources of creativity for you. For example, you might infuse your solutions with the knowledge imparted to you by your culture. This way, your solutions will be characteristically yours. Make a difference by being smart and by being yourself.

Multiple perspectives will enable you to come up with original solutions. You should practice looking at problems from many angles as this will open the floodgate of ideas. Subsequently, you will come up with better solutions.

Mama also suggests that you start using the power of association. This means to link your ideas to an overarching theme or entity. Doing so will help you to not only remember things, but also to communicate your ideas in a more coherent manner. If you are able to associate your thoughts with an external entity which others are acquainted with, they will make the right connections. Doing so will enable them to understand your ideas and solutions, for association often simplifies the process of comprehension. Remember, there are always newer routes to take in life. So if one path does not lead you to the right destination, do not be disheartened; take it as a lesson. Learn as much as you can from any experience and inspire others to do the same by following your vision that is based on kindness and humanity.

The Fair Circus Fare

"Fair is where you get cotton candy."
- Anonymous

Mama hopes that the cotton candy made you aware of the deeper truths about yourself. Herein, you learned how creative solutions of human beings are a result of infusing knowledge (i.e., the sugar of cotton candy) with proper creative attitudes (i.e., the food coloring and the flavor). It is the way that you view your environment, and then help by using your acquired knowledge to come up with original ways of making a difference. Being attentive, using your knowledge, and allowing your creativity to soar, is what will open the floodgates of your potential. This is what will allow you to reach for the stars because for the creative human mind, the sky is the limit.

The more you become aware of your own powers of observation, the more you can put them to good use. Mama wants you to go far in the circus of life. That will only be possible if you allow your imagination to rise above the constraints of a mundane existence. Remember, if you want to be extraordinary, you must break away from the security of your comfort zone. When you do that, you will be able to give back to the world. You will be able to be the person who not only makes a difference, but is the difference. So trust in yourself to be the change that you want to see around you. Mama knows you can do it—and so do you.

Chapter 8

THE CAROUSEL

"Life is like a merry-go-round. It is full of ups and downs, sometimes you feel like you're just going in circles, but when the ride ends, you want to do it again!"

- Linda Poindexter

The Carnival Carousel

You are still walking around the circus, your eyes tracing the spectacle that is eternally unfolding before you. For a suspended moment, the sights of the circus seem to be frozen in time like a vivid painting. It smells like an interactive roadmap and the sounds are like the soft musical notes. This is the time that you want to store in your memory. So you watch the lights that seem to be winking at you, as though you were co-conspirators in some secret mischief. The tang of salty-sweet evening air invades your nose and you feel you could map your entire circus experience from its scents alone. You listen to the peculiar circus music made up of the beats of footsteps and the cadence of people's delighted laughter.

You see the smiling faces of those around you. These are the people who have shared the same time in the circus queue as you. Though some might say it was a coincidence of time and space that put you all in the circus together, you know that the reality goes deeper. It was destined that you spend your time at the circus with the people who are there with you at present. This is how it is in the circus of life. You meet the people you are meant to meet and they enrich your circus experience in ways that you never could have predicted when you first came across them. As you ponder over this truth, your eyes are caught by the rides that, you suddenly think, never stop.

Right now, it is the carousel that grabs your attention. Now that you think about it, you have forever seen the carousel in motion; it is always moving and spinning and wheeling, as though representing life itself. So you stride towards the carousel purposefully, ready to garner deeper lessons from it and interpret it in all the ways you can. No single interpretation is appropriate; you can read the carousel in multiple, even contradictory, ways—for that is often the way to unearth the deepest, truest truths. Remember, it is always your thoughts that give birth to the reality of your life.

Come One, Come All

The carousel's rotating platform is pulsating with life. You approach it, your eyes automatically following the circular motion of the ride. The seats come in the shape of galloping horses that bob up and down, stationary horses and carriages. These are the choices that the riders can select from if they want to ride on the carousel. The entire platform is elaborately decorated with colors splashed generously over every surface—the horses, carriages and the poles that connect them to the platform. The lights shine brightly over the people riding on the carousel, giving them an incandescent appearance. The carousel, comprising of a rotating circular platform, seems to you like a metaphor of life, its unceasing motion signifying the unending movement of existence.

As you get closer to the ride, you have a choice to make: you can either stand on the margins, or you can hop on. This carousel journey is like the journey of life—you can either get in the thick of it or remain standing on the sidelines. Neither of these choices, Mama believes, are necessarily good or bad. The important thing is that you take ownership of the decisions you make regarding your life. By this time in the circus, you are already aware of those aspects of your personality that you were earlier oblivious of. Now, you have come to view the carousel ride as a symbol of life (it gives you the freedom to decide which choice to make).

The people who opt to hop on the ride can be viewed as the adventurous ones. These people throw caution to the wind and leap right into the circle, where all the action is, instead of remaining silent on the edges. Now people who decide to take the ride may go for the galloping horse or for the stable one. The first option, whoever goes for it, will teach them that life, too, has its own vicissitudes. Like the horse that goes up then comes down, life too proceeds in the form of crests and troughs. This is a fact of existence. You would go through highs and lows—the good and the bad times—during the course of your existence. When put together, these highs and lows are what create the patchwork called life.

Then there is the horse that remains stationary. This standing horse, if you go for it, will provide you with relative safety and comfort. It is the more conservative choice to make. By choosing this horse, you will feel more secure than you would on the moving horse. You will be reassured that you are moving—as the carousel continues its rotating motion—but not too vigorously. Your desire for stability and certainty will be fulfilled but at the same time, you will be reassured that you are not stagnant and are going somewhere in life. The carousel experience on this horse can be interpreted as living life, but without giving up on the security that is so important to you.

Then, there is the option of the carriage—by far the most careful and easy route to take. Though a part of the carousel ride, out of all three choices, this is the safest. You can take it if you want to avoid risk. There will be no rocking motion of the horse and you won't have to put yourself out there, as even the stationary horse demands of its rider. In the carriage, you will be seated more comfortably. You will be safe and at the same time, you will be moving. This is the least risky option; the carriage makes no more demands on you than to sit, put your feet up if you like, and watch as the carousel takes you for a little spin.

During the carousel ride, you can learn some essential lessons regarding life. Just like how the carousel is always on the move and never stops for anyone, life keeps moving forward. As you contemplate over the choice of your ride on the carousel, you will see that some people jump headlong into the experience without giving it too much thought. Mama requests that you don't judge them for their haste, for that is merely their way of living. Everyone lives in the way best-suited to their vision of life; we must never use the same yardstick for people, for we are all different from each other.

Then there are people who take a long time to make their choice. They use so much time that the ride might start, leaving them behind to wait for the next round to begin. Now, you might have a problem with this as well. You may be impatient and desire to push them along. To you, the carousel ride does not qualify for a prolonged period of consideration and precaution. However, Mama will again caution that such is the way that they function. No matter how frustrated you are by people's impulsiveness or their premeditation, the choice is all theirs to make.

Still, Mama suggests, you need to strike a balance and avoid being reckless; conversely, do not procrastinate too much, thinking of all that could go wrong. Find a middle way; contemplate, but not too much. Remember, the carousel will not wait for you. Being proactive is important. So you must take the initiative and hop on the ride—going for the option you find best, but in good time. The carousel is for everyone to enjoy. It is inclusive and does not discriminate against whosoever wants to ride it. Remember, this ride is all about having the best time that you can in the circus.

From The Sidelines

When on the carousel platform, you can see all kinds of people who are different from you. Some may be impulsive and some may be the dawdling kind. Then there are those who prefer not to ride the carousel at all. These are the people who make the conscious decision to remain on the sidelines. Though others may judge them for it, they have made that choice for themselves. Mama advises you to find a balance and stick to the middle path.

Mama thinks that even remaining on the sidelines can be used to one's advantage. You see, waiting on the sidelines can be a productive experience, used to indulge in meditation and reflection. Those who are on the margins, rather than on the carousel, can utilize that time—which may seem empty and wasted to others—to contemplate about life, to gain self-awareness and to grow as individuals.

People on the sidelines may be looking at the circus from a different perspective. They may actually be taking a breather before hopping on to the next ride of their choice. It is important to dwell on one's current situation in life; if you recall, this is what Mama asked you to do in the beginning when she suggested that you analyze your life and determine the queue that you are in. Subsequently, it is with people who are standing on the margins, choosing not to jump into the activity hub, that is the carousel, at that point.

Spinning Wheel

As you experience the carousel ride, you will come face to face with your inner reality as you have done throughout the circus. The up and down motion of the horse and the continuous spin of the carousel will remind you of the tumult in your emotional state, and further allow you to confront your problems and dilemmas. Mama hopes that you will use this time to approach your internal battles with a fresh perspective, thereby understanding and resolving them.

When you are on the carousel, you will notice how the blinking lights, the jingling music, and the circular movement of the ride, all trigger a plethora of emotions in you. As you identify your emotions, understand it as a step forward in the right direction.

Mama believes that to be aware of your emotional landscape is an indication that you have matured spiritually, emotionally and psychologically. Once you are able to recognize and name your emotions, which could range from joy and elation to anxiety and fear, you can proceed to the next step, which is to manage these emotions productively.

Sifting through the many emotions that surge through you, you will realize that emotions are seldom cut and dried and each is comprised of many shades. And, being human, you may oscillate between contradictory emotions. The carousel ride will teach you how to better understand the complicated terrain of your emotional existence so you can deal with it in a fruitful manner.

During the dizzying ride, you will also accept the contrast between your internal and external states. You will become conscious of an inner compass within you that is always stable. There may be a continuous churning in your external world, but your private inner compass—denoting your moral and ethical principles—remains secure and steady.

This compass is what shows you the way when you feel directionless. Once you become aware of this compass—courtesy of the contrast provided to you by the shifting carousel—you can clean the dust that may have settled on it. Clear once again, it will enter your consciousness. Now, you can rely on it to lead you in the right direction when the going gets tough. Relying on the compass will help you to trust yourself more; self-reliance, then, will be an added benefit of becoming aware of your inner compass. Mama urges you to locate your compass and to make good use of it.

Carousel Chronicles

There are many stories that will elucidate the carousel experience for you. Mama will relate one of her own to you with the strong hope that you will learn lessons from the story, much like Mama did herself. Mama's daughter, Nora, studies abroad and around the time of her eighteenth birthday, Mama went to visit her. Mama prepared a birthday surprise for her and Nora too, had high expectations from her big day. The day arrived and Mama took Nora and her friend to visit a different city. There, they dined at a fine restaurant, which had been highly recommended to them. The food was great, and so was the dessert. At the end of the dinner, some food was left over, and they asked the waiter to wrap it up so they could give it to a needy person.

Upon inquiry, they found out that it was against the restaurant policy to parcel leftover food. Mama, however, insisted that they do so; you see, a good day should end on a good note, which is what Mama believes. When one is happy, one wants others to be happy too and who knows, the food might provide succour to a hungry person. After Mama explained this to the waiter, he surprisingly agreed to parcel the leftover food. After dinner, Mama took the girls to a nearby amusement park to ride the carousel. There, they were joined by another girl named Fareeda. Mama purchased four tickets for the ride and they all headed to the carousel platform. Once there, they all had to decide which ride to select. Mama told them what she has told you here: the carousel, which represents life, must be enjoyed to the fullest.

Everyone but Fareeda selected the option which appealed to them the most. Fareeda, however, selected the carriage, not the horses. She later explained that she went for the carriage because she had been conditioned into believing that the carousel was not meant for her to enjoy. All four climbed on the carousel and had as much fun as they would allow themselves to have; Mama, at forty years of age, made the most of her time. Fareeda, however, did not. She thought that being a 23-year-old woman, she no longer had the option to partake of the joys of the carousel. She wouldn't allow herself to enjoy the sights and the sounds that make up the carousel experience.

You see, as a girl, she had been taught that it was a taboo for her to let herself have fun on the carousel. When the ride was over and they got off, she had tears running down her face. She gave Mama a big hug, and confided that this was the best time she had ever had in the park. She also confided in Mama that it was not just the carousel ride that she couldn't enjoy, but her entire life had followed the same script to that day. She had allowed herself to be constrained and had never learned to appreciate life and have fun.

This carousel ride was the first time that she had come close to taking delight in any experience. She finally realized that life was not as tough at others make it out to be. This carousel ride effectively transformed her life and she was able to alter her perceptions and by extension, her existence.

Mama related this event to you so you could identify if you too, like Fareeda, have followed a similar pattern in your own life. If so, Mama would urge you to break free from the false limitations that others have placed on you and which you continue to live with. There is time yet for you to take charge of your life and to live it to the fullest—the way it is intended to be lived. The carousel teaches you to appreciate life (i.e., to have fun, to laugh, and to feel happy). Neither age nor anything else, is a limiting factor. The carousel is meant for all, so it is entirely your choice. You can get off the carousel and be unhappy, or get on it with verve and enthusiasm, and proceed to have the time of your life. Mama knows that the moment you make the decision of getting on the carousel will be the moment that you will really start living.

Everybody Rides the Carousel

"I only wanted to tell you that this was the wonderful time for you. Don't let any of it go by without enjoying it. There won't be any more merry-go-rounds. No more cotton candy. No more band concerts. I only wanted to tell you, Martin, that this is the wonderful time. Now! Here! That's all. That's all I wanted to tell you."

- Rod Serling, Stories from the Twilight Zone

By now, Mama hopes that you know how to make the best of your carousel ride. You understand how the carousel is a representation of your life and how it is open to everyone. You have many decisions to take. The first is to get on the ride or to stay on the sidelines. You already know that both routes can be as productive as you want them to be. Once you decide to go on the carousel, you have some other decisions to make, such as choosing between the two horses or the carriage. If you choose to remain on the margin, you have to make it count too. You can take the wait-and-see approach when on the sideline; watch your fellow circus goers and if their carousel experience appeals to you; then you always have the option of going for it yourself.

The carousel also taught you about your emotional state. Moreover, as you learnt about your inner condition, you realized that you had the capacity to manage it effectively. Overall, the carousel ride can prove to be a journey of self-awakening for you. Remember, there is always another ride waiting for you at the end of this one. Once you get off the carousel, you can always get back on it; if that is what you want to do. So do not rush, but allow yourself to really feel the experience. Your time in the circus will bring you in contact with many more interesting encounters. Mama knows these encounters will be fruitful because now you have learned how to get the most out of the queues in your life.

As you enjoy your time on the carousel, Mama wants

you to be fully alive. She wants you to live in the moment. Carpe diem! Seize the day! This is your time and you must make it worthwhile. Make the decisions regarding the carousel on your own and you will realize that the moment that you decide to take on a new path is the moment that you can really start to live life. Appreciate the moment while you still have it. The carousel is not only meant to educate you in the art of self-awareness, but also to apply the knowledge that you have hitherto acquired in the circus. So hop on the carousel if that is what you want. Cherish every minute that you spend on it for that will make all the difference.

Chapter 9

THE JUGGLER

"Life is a juggling act with your own. The trick is to always keep something in your hand and something in the air."

- Chloe Thurlow

A Balancing Act

You have just been on the carousel, spinning round and round, forgetting everything, but being in the moment, living to the fullest, just as you should. Later, you walk around the circus again, feeling liberated from the tyranny of expectations and the curbs that you had imposed on yourself. You now realize that there is more to this circus of life than you ever thought possible. Your mind, you feel, is more open to possibilities now. You know that anything and everything good can happen only if you become receptive to the joys that life offers you at every turn.

Sauntering through the circus again, you think and hope that there may be other marvels for you to discover.

Conversely, you might also be led to think that the circus is done yielding the many wonders that it holds in its magician's hat for you. However, Mama asks you to wait, as there is more to come. You have watched and learned so much about the circus already, and about yourself, but there is another circus act that is waiting to teach you some essential life lessons. So Mama asks you to head towards the circus tent again. There, waiting to unfold before your eyes, is the juggler's act. You know what juggling is. You may even have watched a juggler before, delighted at his capacity to juggle so many objects all at once. However, this time around, you know that you will see beyond the dazzle of the show to the underlying messages in the juggling act.

Now, you will truly focus on the particulars; the beginning of the act, its transition, and its completion. You will also notice the many demands made on the juggler during the act. In short, at this point in the circus, Mama believes that you will start seeing things with your eyes wide open for that is the only way to see things in their entirety. By now, you are aware that everything in this circus is geared to acquaint you with the many aspects of life. You understand that the circus journey is meant to reacquaint you with yourself. As you viewed the various acts performed at the circus, you realized the complexity of life and your own self. You have now begun to see the many layers that make you who you are.

You know that you, as an individual, will find some crucial parallels between yourself and the juggler, in the same way that you have with other elements of the circus. This will grant you yet another perspective with which to look at life. So you refocus your attention on the sight unfolding in the circus ring. Now, your eyes follow the first ball that the juggler flings high up in the air.

Juggling The Jumble

Heralding the performance, the announcer had warned the audience, "Prepare to have your hearts and minds tossed like a lot of coins!"

You laughed at his wit. You see, you didn't expect the juggling act to be so thrilling. You thought it would involve a man hurling balls in the air and catching them in the nick of time. From what you had heard or seen before, it seemed like an act based on chance and probability. A successful catch of the ball could just as easily be an embarrassing drop. As you watch the show now, however, you realize that the juggling act is so much more than you envisaged; requiring far more attention from the juggler than credited.

You can now see that juggling is more than the whirl of balls, the whoosh of the air, or the vertigo it induces in the audience. You watch with bated breath as the juggler juggles many balls in the air. He started out with one bright red ball. Then he added a deep purple one and then a blue one. He juggled the three balls for a while and then, suddenly, threw in three more balls in the mix: green, orange and brown. All the while, the juggler never missed a beat.

Your eyes can barely keep track of the several balls that the juggler is deftly juggling. You do not know where to look: at the juggler or at the balls. The vividly colored balls and their dizzy motion draw your attention; at the same time, you are mesmerized by the juggler. His obvious expertise in juggling so many balls simultaneously, with such self-confidence, amazes you. You wonder how he manages to keep the flow and how the balls never drop to the ground. You see that there is a lot that you can learn from the juggler and so, you get down to the task.

Mama is happy that you are taking the initiative and have become proactive at the circus. The circus only gives up its secrets to those who seek them. So proceed with the sunny hope in your heart that you will find profound meanings hidden behind the juggling act of the circus juggler.

The Juggle Called Life

Do you see how the juggler represents you in your life? Mama wants you to understand that life is a juggling performance in which you are the designated juggler. How do you think that is? Well, have you noticed how many things you have to deal with in life and all at one time? It may be your education, your relationships, or your career, among other pursuits. The bottom line is that there are many responsibilities in your life, and they are all important to you in different degrees, and you need to juggle them successfully for a fulfilling existence. No one would like the many balls being juggled in their lives to come falling down unexpectedly. What everyone desires is that their juggling act remains balanced and successful.

Mama hopes you see how your life resembles a juggling routine. There are always many balls that you have to juggle—some are in your hands and some are in the air. The truth is that you can't have all the balls in your hands at the same time, hence, the juggling. What you have to do is to strike a balance between handling all the different balls of your life. Now, striking a balance demands an understanding of the act of juggling. Mama is here to help you with that. You see, there are two basic tools for juggling that you are in possession of; your hands and your eyes. In the literal act of juggling, you have to have strong hand-eye coordination, good peripheral vision, and quick visual reaction time.

When it comes to the metaphorical act of juggling, there are some more requisite skills required. Mama will first elaborate on the symbolic meaning of the two basic elements of juggling.

The hands that you juggle with can be interpreted as your health, your age, your spirit, or your mental capacity. The juggling hand, in fact, can be all the things that you rely on to function productively in life. Consequently, your hands can be your health, and they can also be your wits; they can be your intelligence and also your brawn. Your soul and your spirit are also your hands. It is essential that your hands remain focused, balanced and strong. Your inner compass that Mama talked about in detail earlier can be your hands too; and for that reason, your compass should be tuned right to serve as a guide for you to manage the several balls of your life. It is thus crucial that the hands you rely on, to juggle the several balls of your life, are strong enough to carry out the task effectively.

The balls of the juggling act called life can be many. These balls depend very much on the queue that you currently occupy in life. It can be said that these balls are representative of the things that you have to manage effectually if you want to live a productive life. So the balls that you have to juggle can be your time, your work and money, your family, your religion, your culture and your tradition. These, as Mama sees it, are what make up the life of human beings. They give significance and meaning to life; accordingly, these are the life balls that must be managed well if you want to be happy.

It is crucial that you understand one fact; at any given time, some balls will be in your hands, and some will be in the air. You must practice 'presence' once again. Presence means that you are focused in the moment, on the ball that you have in your hands. This is the only way you can appreciate all the different, but important aspects of life. If one ball is not valuable to you in one instance, then you can always drop it and focus on the one that is more important. Consider all the juggling balls as opportunities that life has presented you. Appreciate and pay attention to each, for together, they keep the act of life going.

Juggle Through The Muddle

Now, Mama will explain the several balls that you have to juggle in your life. In the circus, you watched the juggler as he juggled many balls—all in different vibrant colors. There were red, purple, blue, green, orange, and brown balls. These balls symbolize the various significant areas of your life essential to enjoy a happy, satisfied existence. To make it clear to you, Mama will consider each colored ball to represent one facet of your life. The red ball stands for your time, the purple one for your work and money, the blue ball for your family, the green one for your religion or spiritual beliefs, the orange one for your culture, and the brown one for the tradition that you have inherited.

The red ball is representative of your time; the red imparts urgency because time is always running out. There are certain periods in your life when you feel that you have plenty of time on your hands. This may be during your break from school or college. Now recall how you spent that time of your life. How did you utilize this resource? Mama views time as the most valuable resource. You only realize the significance of time once you are under pressure. Mama cannot stress enough the importance of using your time wisely, on things that are truly important.

The purple ball that symbolizes your money and work life is equally important. There will be times in your life when you will have a good amount of money; conversely, there will be times when you will be short of money. If you manage your money efficiently when you have it—meaning if you juggle the money ball wisely—then you will have something to fall back on during hard times. If there is a lack of money then you must accept it and spend only on things you need rather than on unnecessary luxuries that you can live without. It is important that you accept the money ball as it is if you want to enjoy what you have in your present.

It is important to maintain a balance at work as well. Work hard in the present so that in the future, which you cannot predict, you have a safety net to rely on. Do not procrastinate but finish today's work today. Don't be lazy but don't be a workaholic either. Maintain a balance at all times. Juggling the work ball along with the blue family ball is imperative. The blue ball—with its connotations of stability, loyalty and trust associated with family—is a fundamental part of one's life. So juggling the blue ball means spending time with your family and being kind and loving towards them. It means to keep a good equilibrium and flow in your relationships with your loved ones.

Make sure to have fun with your family for that is what strengthens your bond with them.

Make No Mistake

There are some balls in a juggler's hands that are trickier. It takes a lot of skill to manage them effectively. In your life, these balls correspond to religion, culture, and tradition. As Mama told you earlier, the green ball stands for your religion. It represents healing, harmony and growth. Mama advises you that whenever you feel confused, you should turn to the source of guidance in your life; your religion. You must, however, approach it with a fair and balanced view; that is what juggling really means. Connecting to your source will allow you to grow and mature as a human being. Juggling this ball well will ensure that your soul is nourished and strengthened.

Since religion impacts your soul, it is important that you understand the nature of this ball clearly. Do not confuse the ball of religion with the other two balls; culture and tradition. Those two are very different balls that you need to juggle with the ball of religion. Understand the orange ball of culture for what it is; the color has connotations of social communication, optimism, warmth, and inclusivity. Appreciating the positive aspects of the culture that you live in is important. However, you must keep your vision clear and your mind open to detect any prejudice that your culture may teach you. Juggling this orange ball requires you to know the difference between right and wrong.

The brown ball, with its connotations of security, protection, comfort, and stability represents tradition. The traditions that you follow keep you anchored, giving meaning to your life. However, juggling this ball means that you understand that tradition is not rigid, though it may seem so. It evolves over time and you must evolve with it. You should not bury yourself in the roots of culture; rather, you must, like a tree, only accept nourishment from it to grow and reach towards the sky. Thus, juggling the ball of tradition is all about learning when to hold on and when to let go. Learn how to handle it and build your capacity to take only the good and leave out the bad from this ball called tradition.

Now, Mama warns you against one pitfall that many stumble into as they juggle the act called life. They fail to understand the difference between the three balls of religion, culture, and tradition. They tend to confuse one with the other and when that happens, the balls come crashing down. Consequently, these unfortunate people develop a limited approach towards life based on this confused mindset. Mama urges you not to grab all three balls at once; to do so would have devastating consequences. It is crucial that you differentiate between these balls and understand the boundaries that demarcate them, managing them wisely to avoid unnecessary complications.

Catch And Drop

"I dropped my juggling balls and my face grew embarrassed. It wasn't until then that I looked around the circus of life and noted all were too consumed on their own juggling act to see. This is when I learned to have fun, and kick the balls instead."

- *Stefanie Schneider*

As you watched the juggling act of the circus, Mama hopes that you learned how to manage the many balls in your life. Juggling requires that you keep yourself focused and pay attention to all the balls that you have to juggle. It also necessitates that you learn to differentiate between the balls because if you don't, you might make a mess of the juggling act. If you mistake one ball for another or if you reach for one ball when you should for another, it will result in a definite drop. If you want to catch all the balls that you are presently juggling at the right time, then you must be completely aware of each ball and its true nature, as well as its importance in your life.

The juggling act of the circus told you that you can always master juggling two balls and then, when you have done that, you can add another, and then another. It all depends on you; Mama believes you have the skill to master the art of juggling many balls at one time. At a young age, the two most important balls are education and time. So Mama asks you to focus on juggling these two efficiently. Then, when you have become skilled at juggling them, you can take up another ball, such as your social skills or an extracurricular activity. It is imperative that you learn to master the balls that you have in your hands at any point of time, instead of taking up more than you can handle. Mama says this because if you don't manage the balls properly and even if one falls, it would affect the entire juggling act.

Mastering the juggling act means to know which balls to include in your juggling act of life. It means to know everything about these balls so that the act doesn't collapse around you. It also means to maneuver your way intelligently and positively through the juggling process to ensure success. There will be many people who will have the same or similar balls to juggle in life. They too, will have work, family, religion, and many of the other juggling balls that you do. However, everyone will continue differently. Do not try to imitate others, and focus on being yourself. You are the only person who can juggle the act of your life in the best way possible.

Sometimes in life, we should elect to ride the carriage and let others lead. We do not need to be leaders all the time, nor should we engage ourselves in other people's battles. We should take a seat and view life as a bystander. Alternatively, those who elect the horse should opt to take the lead in their lives and not allow others to hijack their reins.

You are unique; your juggling act is unique as well. So embrace your uniqueness for it makes you who you are. Mama wants you to work hard at maintaining your individuality—it is what sets you apart from the millions. Juggle your way through life with optimism and determination. Be fully present in the moments of juggling, and remember to have fun as well. That is the whole essence and purpose of the juggle called life. The main lesson that Mama wants you to take away now is to believe in yourself. Once you do that, you will see how brilliantly and successfully you perform in this juggling act of the circus called life.

Chapter 10

THE MUSIC

"Music gives a soul to the universe, wings to the mind, flight to the imagination and life to everything."

- Plato

The Songs Of The Circus

As you make your way from one circus attraction to another, your ears are flooded with the rise and fall of music. Everywhere you go, you hear the beats and rhythms. The pulses and the cadence of the songs the circus plays for you drum in your ears. When you pay attention, the music seems very particular to each act of the circus. On the carousel, you hear a different music than you do at the juggler's show; the soundtrack to which the dancers dance is not the same as that during the trapeze performance. And now, at this point in the circus, you have realized that there is more to the music of each act than appears on the surface.

To people who have not yet learned to discern the multi-layered nature of the circus, the music of each performance may not hold much essence. You, coming far in your thought, may know that nothing in the circus is based on chance. The circus music is hardly a result of a coin tossup. You know that the music is not random or accidental, but a well thought-out and an integral part of the performance and the circus experience. The music is carefully selected to complement each act, not take away from it in any way. The music sometimes recedes into the background; at other times, it progresses to the foreground, and guides you through the circus. In both cases, the music of the circus has an undeniable and vital presence, without which your time here would be incomplete.

The music of the circus may be your guide on this journey. It can decide the course of your circus trip and take you to unplanned places. To illustrate this, let's say you were heading towards the contortionist's act when you heard the faint, but unmistakable notes of some upbeat music playing. Drawn by the positive mood the music evoked in you, you diverted your path towards a circus act that was not on your agenda. This new act turned out to be better than anything else you had watched so far; it may have taught you lessons, profound and meaningful, about yourself. So, you see, changing the road made all the difference.

And what was behind it all? The music that you heard, right?

Keeping that in mind, take Mama's hand now. Come with her to decipher the songs of the circus and what they could mean for you.

The Duet Of Life

As you listen to the music around you—really listen, and pay attention—you begin to comprehend some basic facts about the music of your own life. Just as the background score of each circus act is different from the next, you begin to see that the music of your life is entirely different from that of the next person. Even so, the common denominator between the people of the world is music. It is a universal language that speaks to everyone, regardless of age, race, religion or culture. In fact, music can be said to be one of the few elements that unites rather than separates people. Even animals understand music. The impact of music on our lives cannot be denied.

In broad terms, there are two types of music that we dance to; the music inside and the music outside. To put it simply, first, there is your internal music that is your own and is highly specific to you; it is subject to your nature and temperament. Then, there is the external music that lies outside of you and is independent of you; yet it accompanies you all through your life and you cannot exist without it. The most important thing, Mama advises, is to maintain harmony between your inner music and the one that is external to you. You must understand how they both work in tandem to make up the soundtrack of your life.

The first step to do that is to understand what internal music really is.

The Beats Of The Heart

It is important to listen to the music inside of you. The internal notes that play within each person are unique; they are distinct and specific to them. This music represents the passion that resides within you. The tune that plays inside you is your inner guide, your compass, that shows you the way; much like the circus music. The course of your life is governed by this inner music, its rhythms, and its rhymes. So it is only logical that you understand it better. Knowing yourself means learning the musical notes that you live your life by, often unconsciously.

Once you become acquainted with your inner music, it will become easier for you to become the conductor of the orchestra of your life. You will be able to tweak the inner strings of your heart to create a more beautiful tune and become a better person. Your inner music can be your source of peace. And when that happens, the music within you can reverberate to those around you to impact them positively. Enjoying and appreciating life and living it to the fullest is what determines your inner music.

Your inner music can drive you to become a better human being. Conversely, it can wreak havoc in your life if you do not implement timely changes. For example, due to the external circumstances of your life, your internal music may be altered. The music of your mind might overpower the music of your heart. This mind music might tell you to worry, to calculate, and to look at things from a rational perspective. On the other hand, the music of the heart will tell you to slow down, take a deep breath, and be yourself.

Mama urges you to listen to the music of your heart rather than that of your mind, as the former follows your true instinct while the latter often amends itself to meet others' expectations of you. In this sense, the heart's music can be called your inner music notes and the mind's music can be termed the external notes. The internal music notes concern the matters of the heart. They are about optimism and hopefulness. On the other hand, the external music notes follow the reasoning and logic that the external world constantly feeds you. Your internal musical notes are higher and louder than the external ones. These, then, are the notes that you must follow if you wish to live a content life.

The Synching Act

The most important aspect, as Mama alluded to earlier, is that you maintain harmony between your internal and external notes. So make sure to synchronize the two; this is the only way to guarantee that the music of your life remains in tune, not discordant. Let your inner music be your primary guide. Do not let the external music notes overwhelm you. For instance, sometimes your inner music may be upbeat and positive, but you encounter a person whose heart's music is sad and depressing. Won't the music of one person impact that of the other?

What could happen is that the person who is out of tune with their inner music may let the upbeat person's music engulf them. If the person with the happy rhythm is in sync with their internal music notes, their radiating positive energy can lift the other person out of his or her depresssed state. The louder and stronger music note will always affect the other person's notes and force them to synchronize their rhythm to the higher note rhythm.

Furthermore, your internal music notes, by nature, are louder and more consistent; they are what drive you to the ultimate destination, which is love. So learn how to be in sync with your inner music notes. What does it really mean to be in tune with your own rhythm? Mama says it means that you have reached an internal balance relative to your age, environment, and surroundings. This leads you to create harmony and maintain your internal balance.

It's like sitting on the beach alone, watching the waves pounding the sand. Your meditation, coupled with your balanced internal rhythm, will actually make your internal note higher. Similarly, if you are sad, your overall internal rhythmic note will go lower.

Either way, you must understand and be in sync with your internal note, because it is your real compass in life.

Even if you are sad and reflecting over your worries, once you sit at the beach and start watching the waves, your sorrows will begin to subside. They will be washed away by the rising and falling waves. You will soon realize the message being conveyed by the waves: that like everything else in life, sorrows also come and go. As you sit at the beach and confront your sorrows, the beat of the ocean and the crescendo of the waves work with you in tandem to dissolve your low tide in a magical way. You will learn to accept that nothing on this earth is created to last.

A Universal Language

As you already understand, music is a universal language with three core objectives; love, peace, and beauty. These are the abstracts that propel and give rise to music. The world around us represents a universal musical note with its three pillars of love, beauty and peace. Every act in the world has either one, or all of these three, as underlying motivators.

Consider the musical note of love, which is accounted by many as an act carried out by individuals and nations alike. For example, an act of war against an enemy country is born out of the love for one's own country, yet it ends in destruction on both sides. Even though the outcome often belies the cause, the truth prevails that love was the underlying reason and thus, the source of the musical note. Now you need to determine which musical note is the source of your actions. Decide which note you want to follow in life and be very particular about it. Take time to reflect if your actions, though born out of love, engender peace. Answer that question before committing any act to avoid adverse consequences. To do otherwise will mean destroying the harmony of the universal musical tone.

Address also the pillar of beauty. Consider this: if you cut down a tree, does it result in beauty or ugliness? You tear down a house. Is the result beautiful or ugly? It depends on the end result and the purpose, right? Keeping this in mind, Mama asks you to think before you perform any act. If your actions result in ugliness rather than in beauty, then you must stop immediately. Doing otherwise will not only upset the balance of the external world, but will also disturb your inner harmony and balance, causing you unnecessary pain.

The key is to be aware of which musical note to follow in life. It is only logical that you follow the music of the universe, which promotes love, peace and beauty. This is the true calling of Mother Earth. You must be judicious in making the right decision, which must be in harmony with your inner music.

Once you hit the right sync between your inner music notes and the outer ones, you will begin to recognize the notes that are discordant. Then all the news reports about war and destruction will strike you as cacophonous. Your inner music will confirm that for you. You will begin to not just see, but feel how wrong these acts are because they disrupt the coherence of the universal musical note.

Accordingly, undertake this task of increasing your self-awareness by synchronizing yourself with the musical notes of love, peace and beauty. Open your eyes to the world and start seeing the true nature of everything to identify it as musical or dissonant. Let the three pillars or core aspects of music be your internal compass. Follow them as you make your way through this circus so that you become mindful of both, the obvious and the subtle beats of the circus music.

The Lyrics

You might be someone who listens to music often. You might listen to music of various kinds just to keep up with friends, or some trend, or it may, truly, be your passion. However, what often happens is that you end up listening to only the music at the cost of the lyrics. It is time that you start paying attention to the words of the songs you listen to because, though you might not realize it, they unconsciously affect you. If the message encoded in those songs is, for example, regressive or detrimental to your mental health, then in time, it will begin to influence you. Eventually, the message might even become a belief that you subconsciously hold and actively act on.

Negative messages in lyrics can reinforce pessimistic feelings. Replaying the same song with the same damaging lyrics means repeating the same thoughts to yourself. It is then only a matter of time before you start believing their content, and then living them out as well. For example, if the lyrics of a song are racist or abusive, you might adopt those words in your language and attitude. You might then also internalize the meaning behind those words, which would alter and disrupt your inner harmony.

Take another example; you might listen to songs that convey the message of pain over and over again, so much so that you internalized the message. In time, you might begin to relate to the pain. To the point that your subconscious will tell you, "I've heard it so many times, and now I believe that there is merely the feeling of pain for me to experience." Do you see how detrimental this will be for you? So to avoid such an outcome, Mama advises you to be careful in your music selection. Choose to listen to music with lyrics that lift you up rather than pull you down. Do not take lightly the power of the underlying message in each song. Go for the music that will leave you with a strong sense of self-belief. This has been the primary purpose of the circus journey; to empower you to be the best version of yourself. In this regard, music and its lyrics play an integral role. Choose wisely because your decision will make a difference to your future.

Find The Tempo

Mama knows that at this point in the circus, you are well aware of the need to keep your internal music rhythm synchronized with the external music rhythm. You realize now that this is the way for you to find and maintain a balance between yourself and the world around you. Being at harmony with your surroundings means you possess the right tools to manage and control the vibes that you receive from the external world. It also means that you now have the ability to synchronize with people of your choice.

You see, when you are not in tune with yourself, you become vulnerable to being overwhelmed by other people's music, as was earlier illustrated. However, when you are in sync with yourself, you will realize which people will influence you and which won't. With the right knowledge, you can make the correct choice and only choose to sync with those who bring out the best in you, who enrich your inner life, and exclude those who sap you of your energy and leave you feeling depleted. Sync with people who share your dreams and visions and are in rhythm with you.

Let your inner compass be your guide. It will help you choose what will uplift you and help you to soar high. It will also help you avoid the pits and those people that will drag you down. In time, you will begin to realize that friends who are in sync with you, may however interpret the music differently. You will begin to see how everyone comprehends music in their own specific way. Some might feel more in tune with one particular beat, lyrics and rhythm, while others might not. You will begin to understand that even those you are in sync with are unique in their own way and everyone sways to their own music.

You can find clues regarding your own emotional state by assessing the music that you listen to. For example, if you have been listening to angry rap lately, it might indicate your current inner turbulence and anger. The truth of what you feel within can be discerned by the music you are drawn to, for at such times, your inner music will seek external music that it is attuned to. This, then, can become a starting point for you to understand your own feelings and emotions.

Thus, music can become a way to work through your internal conflict. It can become a way for you to understand and then accept yourself. This will eventually allow you to let go of the negative feelings you had been holding on to for so long. In time, you will come to terms with yourself and your inner state, reclaiming the balance you had earlier lost. You can see the impact of music on you. Since it speaks to everyone, music can be a way of communicating at several levels. Make use of this to find the right tempo to live your life. Find the rhythm and the beat. In time, your internal music note will unfold to guide you through life and help you live it the way you want to.

The Cadence of Life

"Music expresses that which cannot be said and on which it is impossible to be silent."

- Victor Hugo

Mama is happy that you understand what circus music is all about. She now wants you to become conscious of the kind of music you listen to, for music always has a message for you. You will, if you pay attention, not just understand the message, but why you are drawn to that particular type of music. Music can act as a catalyst to let your inner self unfold. As you walk through the circus while listening to its music, which changes at every turn, you begin to realize what your inner self is trying to tell you. Music can help you understand yourself by translating the message that often gets muffled by the noise around you. Get rid of this noise as it prevents you from listening to yourself, and your own heartbeat.

In the space between musical notes and silence, you can finally begin to hear your inner voice. Music has the power to transpose you to a different time; it might take you back to happy times in the past or it may carry you forward, dreaming of a brighter future. You move on from one music piece to the next—the notes will change, but the music will remain constant. So fully immerse yourself in the music that you hear—both internal and external. Find joy in it and if it makes you happy, share it with others so they can feel happy as well.

You must also ensure that you allow others to live by their inner music notes and do not infringe on their right to do so. Do not let music that is out of sync with you to take over you, especially when this music is detrimental to your growth. Remember, each of us has a different melody that holds sway over us. Respect other people's music so they return the favor to you.

So in this chapter, you discovered all about your internal music and the music that is external to you. You also learned how important it is for you to find a balance between the two. Mama also told you how vital it is to pay close attention to your inner music and to follow its beat and rhythm if you want to have a satisfying life. Bring yourself in tune with your inner musical notes to find your way to peace, love and beauty. This is how Mama believes you can learn the art of self-awareness.

Also, you learned how you must never forget to focus on the lyrics of the songs that you listen to. As Mama explained, the messages programmed into song lyrics can alter your inner state, consciously or subconsciously. Then, become aware of the musical notes that others send your way; accept only those notes that are optimistic, and in tune with your internal music. Do not let yourself be overtaken by another person's tune, which is out of sync with yours. Always sync with the right person, whose notes are in harmony with yours, for it can make a positive difference in your life.

Mama wants you to revel in music, for it is a universal

joy. You know now how music brings people from all walks of life together. How amazing is it that people do not even need to talk to appreciate and love each other? How wonderful would it be if, under the umbrella of music, the entire world could join hands and become one! Such is the power of music, so bring yourself in tune with your inner music as well as the external one. You will see for yourself how music can inspire you and give you happiness, as well as hope for a better future.

Chapter 11

THE TIGHTROPE

"Life is like walking a tightrope:
A balance between turning inward
Often enough to find your happy core
And focusing outward
Often enough to care a little more.
Leaning too much inward
May make you aloof and narcissistic
Leaning too much outward
May make you bitter and pessimistic.
Keeping balance fuels life with hope."

- Joan Marques

Tightrope Time

In the center of the circus, there is a large tent rising high up, as though it wants to touch the sky. It is a large tent, and you can already tell it's one of the main circus attractions that draws people like a magnet. There are so many people who want to watch this act that only admits audiences on a 'first come, first serve' basis. You make your way into this tent and as you enter behind your fellow circus goers, you find that this indeed is a place where main circus events take place. The tent is packed with people, all anticipating the next act of the circus; the tightrope. You can see why they are so excited, because you are just as enthusiastic as they are. There is something fascinating about tightrope artists; as they seem to walk effortlessly on air, defying gravity with such aplomb.

Suddenly, the lights are dimmed and only a bright spotlight is trained towards the center of the stage. Then, your attention is trained towards the announcer's voice, declaring the tightrope act is about to begin.

He says to the audience jokingly, "Tighten your seatbelts, folks! This show will make you feel as though you were sitting on the sky-edge, and with a single step wrong, you'd fall down, down, down…!"

The audience laughs and cannot wait to experience this vicarious thrill. You, along with all the others, watch as the the performers begin to appear. The act you could not wait for has begun.

The Tightrope Of Life

You watch with your eyes wide open as the funambulists—meaning the tightrope walkers—begin their breathtaking performance. Your gaze follows one artist as he begins to proceed assuredly along the tight wire that is affixed between two stands. He extends his arms out, as though they were wings. You figure that he does so to maintain his balance on the thin rope. He takes quick steps forward, looking straight ahead. The grace with which he walks makes one feel as though he were walking along a garden path rather than on a thin wire hanging several feet above the ground.

As you observe the performance, you are amazed at his courage, but most of all you are inspired by his immaculate sense of balance. You ask yourself just how he manages to be suspended in air and walk as though it was no great feat? Soon, all that you have learned in your time at the circus helps you understand the act of the tightrope. You begin to connect the dots and see how the tightrope is a metaphor for life. You start to see how life itself is a balancing act. Just as the tightrope act of the circus is about walking a rope, while maintaining your balance, life is an act where you have to sustain your balance if you want to make a success out of it.

There are so many things that we do in our lives, all of which, be they work or personal, vie for our attention. Often, we compromise one activity for the other, though both may be equally important. Think about it: isn't work life important? But family life is equally so. Can you let go of one entirely for the other? Obviously not! So what can you do to give your best to all that you have on your plate? The key to that,

Mama feels, is to strike a balance.

Often, life can get so hectic that you end up feeling as though you were hanging by a thread. Under such circumstances, finding the right balance is what would make you walk over the tightrope of life, with the certainty of a tightrope walker.

You must know from the outset that tightrope walking is a demanding, strenuous task. It will be tough at first. No tightrope walker ever perfected the art of walking on a thin rope without stumbling during practice and sustaining some bruises. You, too, will need to work at attaining balance in your life. Mama cautions that you will learn by trial and error; you will make mistakes and that is all right. You are expected to fall. However, you must get back up on your feet and resume walking the rope with the same determination. That would indicate your true commitment to learn the balancing act of life. There are some tools that you can use to help you walk the tightrope of life. Mama will elaborate on those now.

Tools Of The Tightrope Walk

In the circus of life, you live within certain frameworks. You can always use these as tools to guide your way on the tightrope as you attempt to maintain your balance. These tools include your culture and tradition. You can rely on them to find your balance, for they can prove to be beneficial in many ways. However, you also need to keep your eyes open and look out for those aspects in your culture that might compromise your balance on the tightrope—either by holding you back or by upsetting your equilibrium. You need to realize when that happens, so you can take measures to do what is best for you.

In many countries, culture is more an impediment to, rather than a catalyst for personal transformation. Despite your being a unique individual, it can set limits on you, constricting you and forcing you into a preexisting mold. For example, in the Arab world, gender roles prevail, even at workplaces, where women are restricted from doing certain jobs, though they may have a passion and be well-qualified for it. Societal taboos that are in place are enough to induce them to alter their beliefs, behavior, ambitions and goals to fit in and be accepted by society.

Time and again, people confuse culture and tradition. Culture reflects the characteristics that describe a society at a particular time and is mostly associated with art forms, whereas tradition refers to the beliefs and behaviors that are passed down, within a group or society, from one generation to the next. Though tradition and culture often go hand in hand, there are differences between the two. You can live in different cultures throughout your life, yet if you hold on fast to the traditions that you have inherited, you will remain stuck in the same old mindset instead of allowing your mind to roam free, broaden its thinking and absorb new ideas.

Mama wants you to adapt to the different cultures,

instead of resisting change and being rigid. Change and adaptation are signs of life. Therefore, when exposed to a different culture or even while living amidst your own culture, you must find individual ways to thrive and grow. You must capitalize on the advantages that any culture offers you but at the same time, you must avoid those beliefs and practices that may put you at a disadvantage when compared to the rest of the world. Make it a point to learn as much as you can for that is what will help you improve yourself. The more you know, the better choices you can make. It all depends on how you receive and use the information that the world sends your way.

Most cultures are dependent on religion. This reflects in the way they think, act and react to situations. Religion acts as their moral compass; it is also true that right or wrong is determined by various cultures in different ways. Therefore, when it comes to relying on cultural frameworks, Mama asks you to exercise your own intellect. You must sift through things, trace them back to their source, and find out whether the directions and orders issued to you are relevant or not. Then, and only then, must you abide by them.

Always make it a point to evaluate norms because cultures are relative in nature and can be wrong, as much as they can be right, about life. There may be times when you will find yourself at crossroads, not knowing which path to take. However, a balanced mind, sharpened by critical thinking, will take the right decision. You, too, will be able to do that if you learn the balancing act of life and are brave enough to go against the norm.

Be The Change

In life, you may feel forced to go where others are going. You may feel compelled to conform because others do not see your uniqueness. As you have experienced the various acts of the circus, you have learnt to look for the deeper meanings behind everything you encounter. You might want to change the world now, to modify certain practices to make the world a better place. Yet, you may be held back by culture or society, with its fixed ideas about who you should or should not be. In that case, Mama advises you to take the first step and bring about the change that you desire.

The truth is that people live entirely in the here and now, without envisaging how the world can be made better for future generations. They are unwilling to accept visionaries, because their ideas seem as dangerous to them as a tightrope acts. Such people want a comfortable, risk-free life, with minimum changes. They forget that the greatest inventions of the world began with a wild idea which was ridiculed and rejected by the society of the time.

So, Mama advises you to persist in your dreams and chase them proactively. Though people around you will try to warn you, apparently concerned for your wellbeing, the truth is that the same was said to all tightrope walkers. They wouldn't be performing so mesmerizingly before your eyes if they had heeded the counsel of such people who are afraid and wary of change. Though your dream project may be novel, think of yourself as a pioneer who is showing others the way. Be as daring with your dreams as a tightrope walker and inspire others to share in your dreams and to follow their own dreams as well. In short, do not be afraid of the changes taking place around you – rather, be the change that you want to see in the world.

Instruments Of Balance

There are many other tools that you can use to perfect your balancing act in life. Though walking on this tightrope is not easy, there are ways that you can maintain your balance. Mama will tell you several of those so you can perhaps adopt them and see how they impact the balance of your life.

Among the most important elements of your life are your habits. Your habits can make or break you. Changing your habits positively can be a quick-fire way to regain the balance that you may have lost in life. Now, use this time to take a brief survey of the habits by which you live your life. Analyze them and try to determine whether they help you maintain a balance in your life or if they destabilize your life at every turn. Your habits become wired into your brain because you repeat them daily. Evaluating your habits allows you to develop good new ones and use them to strike the right balance in your life. In time, you will begin to act on them automatically. Take, for example, the habit of drinking plenty of water in a day. You know drinking a good amount of water is beneficial to your health, yet you somehow never manage to remember or find the time to enforce it. If you consciously develop this habit of drinking sufficient water daily, or of exercising on certain days, your brain will become programmed to perform these tasks automatically.

You can also develop good interpersonal habits so that they become a part of your routine. For example, you can begin your day by greeting your family with a smile and end the day by hugging them. These actions will evoke positive feelings between yourself and your family members, improving your mood and psychological welfare, as well as theirs. Once you get into the habit, your brain will prompt you automatically so you do not forget. You will send out good vibes, and good vibes will find their way back to you.

Then you can strike a psychological balance for yourself by stopping yourself from fixating on the negatives. You can do this by developing the habit of gratitude. This is a habit that will refocus your attention on the blessings that you have in life. Mama will tell you that there are things in your life that you have never noticed and that you might take for granted. So cultivate the habit of gratitude; as psychology proves it, appreciating the good things in your life will make you feel happier. It will also increase your empathy and make you more optimistic. You will find equilibrium in life where you are able to be thankful for the things that you have while at the same time, you are motivated to work towards your goals.

Yet another habit you can work on is your sleep pattern. The significance of sleeping habits, and their impact on one's overall health and wellbeing, is often ignored. Mama wishes that you pay attention to this aspect of your life. Improve your sleeping habit, go to sleep at a specific time and for enough hours so that you wake up feeling refreshed. This will provide you the energy required to face the day ahead. Develop some triggers that will help you fall asleep. Your brain can be programmed through repeated actions, to associate certain practices with your sleep time. For example, you can use a specific aroma every day before you go to bed; in time, your brain will associate the scent with your sleep time and you will find it easier to fall asleep at the specific time when you use that fragrance.

Furthermore, you can develop the habit of meditation to relieve mental strain. You can practice relaxation techniques or breathing exercises that will help you unwind after a tiring day. You can use this as your personal time to get in touch with your inner soul. In a relaxed state, you can let go of the day's worries and review problems with more clarity. Your judgement will no longer be clouded and you will find yourself in a healthier, more balanced frame of mind. These are some of the tools you can use to find the right balance on the tightrope of life. Mama has given you a headstart and she now trusts you to customize the tools and even come up with new ways to balance your life. You know that you can do it, and so does she.

The Creative Spark

Another way for you to find balance in life is to explore your creative side. All of us have a creative spark, only that it gets suppressed as we age, especially in societies that prize conventionality and playing by the rules. In the circus, after beholding so many creative acts, Mama is sure you now want to explore your own creativity. Mama is sure that you can use your creativity to balance out the multitude of practical things that you have to do in your daily life. Our routines are structured in ways that leave us little room to be spontaneous. Though there are flashes of creativity, we end up quashing them to be more 'realistic' and 'level-headed'.

What a lot of people don't know is that creativity can do wonders for their wellbeing, as well as promote their productivity. In that sense, any creative act can help you relax. It can stimulate your brain to be more innovative and imaginative. It can help you express yourself to others while at the same time, it can help you understand yourself better as you work through the creative process. You can either draw or write. Just let yourself be yourself; give up all thoughts of impressing others or getting their approval. Do your creative acts only for yourself first.

You can write your thoughts down freely on paper without modifying them. The process of free writing will help you get your thoughts out of your system and view them objectively. After using writing as an act of purgation, you will feel lighter and also find the balance that you thought you had lost. Young people are vulnerable and can be affected by negativity; they can also let their own insecurities overwhelm them. You, at your young age, can use your own creativity to assess your own feelings and understand them better. Let your creative juices flow, enabling you to think outside the box. Eventually, creativity will become a way of life.

Mama has her own personal routine that she uses to restore balance in her life. Since Mama is a religious person, she has made a habit of conversing with God daily. This technique involves writing three papers every morning about what is happening in her life and what she wants in terms of worldly and spiritual things. Then she conveys those messages to God. This process of meditation and sublimation is profound in that it leaves Mama with a rediscovered clarity of vision and peace of mind.

Yet another 'creative' technique that can spur growth is to celebrate your mistakes. Mama advocates this method for the benefits it can bestow on you, as well as on those around you. Being a human, you make mistakes in life. However, denying those mistakes or feeling ashamed about them only gives impetus to the cycle of negativity. What Mama suggests is that you take a creative route when it comes to admitting your mistakes. Any time that you make a mistake, just talk about it with other people. Consider that committing the mistake has left you better than before. With your productive mindset, Mama believes you now use your mistakes to learn from them. Tell others so as to inform them not to make similar mistakes. This will make sure that you not just learn from others, but also do your part by teaching them how to be better versions of themselves.

The Real World Tightrope

You are surrounded by people who have performed so many feats in life. Make it a point to ask people about their experiences. Seek out those who have been creative and daring. When you ask them about their life experiences, you will gain knowledge from them. Anyone can go to the internet and type keywords into the Google search bar, but that is a remote way of learning. Mama prefers learning from someone who has had a hands-on experience rather than from the internet, and would advise you to do the same. When you talk to people, you will find out how they have lived their lives. From listening to their stories, you will learn things first-hand on a personal scale. This will help you acquire understanding that is more in-depth and sound.

During the tightrope of life, there will be many distractions, but you can't let them get in your way.

Remember, you are walking on a tightrope, which demands all your attention. These distractions come in the form of luxuries that you don't need, but which the world requires you to possess. Though they may serve no real purpose in your life, yet you might find yourself running after them. This will disturb your financial equilibrium. You do not need to go after things that you do not need. Your focus on the tightrope act will be made easier if you realize you already have everything you need. Learn to perfect this balancing act by knowing how to invest your money, for it can make a big difference in your life down the line.

Be grateful for the things you do have in life. Your basic requirements for survival are food and water. Take note of all that you already have around you. Enjoy those as blessings and share them with your loved ones. Make informed choices and do not just blindly follow the herd. Maintain a balance in your life by holding beliefs that are conducive to growth. Do not adopt other people's beliefs blindly, but use your own intelligence to decipher what suits you best and follow that. Remember, this life of yours is an act only you can balance. If you leave it to others by letting them unwittingly do what they do, it will collapse like a house of cards.

The Tale Of Tightropes

"Life is like walking on a tightrope. We are sure to fall if we keep looking behind instead of at what is ahead."

- Master Cheng Yen

As you made your way through the tightrope act of the circus, you learned how life, too, resembles a tightrope act. Mama showed you how you can make the best of the tightrope of life by using various tools to maintain your balance. It is important for you to strike the right balance by focusing on things that will take you forward in life. You can rely on your culture to guide you but as Mama has told you, it is important that you use your own judgement to do what is right for you. After all, we are all different people with different needs.

Mama also explained to you how you can restore balance in your life by adopting habits that will positively impact your daily routine. Form and establish healthy habits to find the right equilibrium. You can learn about yourself by giving free rein to your creative nature instead of suppressing it. Contrariwise, you can broaden your outlook by listening to others' experiences. Gaining knowledge is vital; just like a seed, if you water it with your passion to learn more, it will grow into a tree. Though it may take you some time to mature and perfect the art of balancing your life, Mama reassures you that each of us matures as per our own timeline, so do not rush the process.

Be yourself, because only you can strike the right balance in your life. So even though you listen to others and learn from your culture and traditions, make sure to keep an open mind. Find new perspectives and try to understand things profoundly. You will gain insight into how things really work as you grow on this circus journey. In time, you will understand what to focus on and what to disregard. Just extend your arms like a tightrope artist and walk confidently along the length of the life rope. Take joy in all that you do and remember to be your own person because it is fun being you!

Chapter 12

THE HULA HOOP

"The hoop is there to remind us not to jump through it, not to submit to someone else's control."

- Kit Williams

Hula Hooping Show

The next show of the circus is the hula hoop. You have to wait for a while for this show to begin though. The euphoria of the tightrope act still grips you and your fellow circus goers inside the tent, where the circus music adds to the elevated mood. You feel a sense of camaraderie because they have accompanied you through your circus journey. Though you have shared experiences with them, the circus has been an individual journey for you. As you chat with these people whom you have shared the various queues with, you feel very much present in the moment. You know that this is a time to cherish because soon, it will become a fond memory.

You hear the announcer herald the beginning of the hula hoop show. Only the stage lights shine bright while the rest are dimmed. You watch in anticipation, as several hula hoop artists make their way to the center of the platform. The hula hoop act has long fascinated you and now, professional artists will perform right before your eyes. There are many performers; some with one hoop, others with more. The show has now begun.

The Hula Hoop Of Life

You watch as the artists place their hoops on the ground, bowing with fanfare to the delight of the excited audience. Then, they reach down and grab their hoops by the edges pulling them up to their waists. The artists begin by swinging the hoops lightly, matching the rhythm of the music blaring from the speakers. Many times during the act, you think the hula hoops might drop to the ground, yet the artists know how to keep the performance going. Not once do the hula hoops fall; they just run up and down the bodies of the performers effortlessly. The movement of the performers is smooth, almost fluid, and you can't help but applaud their control of the hoops.

The hula hoop performance represents the hula hooping act that is life. The performance can teach you a lot about living, as life, too, has its numerous and varied hula hoops. Like the performers on stage, there are many hoops in your life that you have to spin without letting them drop to the ground. You have been performing the act instinctively, but now, you realise that learning more about it will help you perfect the art of hula hooping. Mama is here to teach you this art, which will benefit you as much as the other acts have.

While the performers twirl the hoops around their swaying bodies, you begin to look for the deeper insights behind the elaborate performance. You already notice that some artists have more hoops than others, while some perform tricks in addition to balancing the hoop around their bodies. You observe their control of the hoops and feel that they truly are masters of this game. You decide to be as good at controlling the hoops of your life as the hula hoop performers on the stage. But for that to happen, you first have to get hold of those hoops. You have to find out what those hoops are to work best with them. So take Mama's hand and listen to her as she tells you about the hoops of your life.

Looping Through The Hoops

The hoops of your life are the various things that you have on your plate. Your family can be a hoop and your friends can be another hoop for you to tackle. Your hobbies are a hoop, and your worries and anxieties are also a hoop. You have to manage several hoops in your life. Sometimes, there is just one hoop that takes precedence while at other times, you have to work with several hoops at one time. You work hard to keep moving with the hoops so they do not fall down.

You know what it's like, though. Sometimes, the various hoops of your life can really try your patience and take a toll on your strength. The trick with the hoops, Mama recommends, is to move with them. Instead of trying to overpower the hoop, you have to go along with it before you can finally manage it. Swinging the hoop around your body is a demanding task; you have to swing it and also sway with it. You can't stay still if you want the hoop to move. You can't be too slow, or the hoop won't gain any momentum at all. Conversely, you can't move too fast for that will definitely cause the hoop to clatter down your legs to the ground. So what is it that you can do to make your hooping a smooth, uninterrupted process?

For a successful hula hooping act, you need to make sure that you know which hoops you are tackling. You cannot have a hoop that is too big for you, nor one that is too small. The hoop has to fit you or you won't even begin to hula hoop. It is also a fact that through the act of hooping, the hoops end up having a lasting effect on you. They, in simple terms, shape you. In other words, while you swing the hoops, they will leave their impact on you. Now, the hoops of your life can have a positive effect on you, but they can also have a negative effect. You can decide what results the hoops leave on you, and to what extent, if you resolve to manage them efficiently.

If you think about it, the hula hoop act revolves around a performer who passes the hula hoop from his head, down to his torso, and all the way to his legs. He swings the hoop around his body, swirls it down to his feet, and then up again. The hula hoop is not attached to any string. It is free from all sorts of trappings. You can say that the hoop, being free from any links or threads, becomes a symbol of liberation. Through hula hooping, you can learn to liberate yourself from any ties; especifically the ones that do not allow you to be yourself. This is one of the messages to be taken away from the act of hula hooping; that you can free yourself from any attachments that are restrictive.

Think of any relations or connections in your life, be they to people or things or traditions, which are limiting or downright harmful for you. They can be friends or associates, who make you doubt yourself or restrain you from following your dreams. What would you do under such circumstances? Would you allow them to influence you and continue your association with them, or would you take a step back to take stock of the situation?

Mama suggests that you try and distance yourself from such people so that you can address the issue objectively. You cannot do that if you are tied to them emotionally or physically. You need to free yourself, just like a hula hoop, and see where you can go on your own. As you watch the hula hoop artists, you can tell that the hoop sometimes has a will of its own. You need to do the same if you want to live life on your own terms. In your lifetime, you will encounter people who will put you down. They will question you, ridicule you, and be condescending towards you. They will tell you that you are incapable. Often, such people will come to you in the guise of friends and well-wishers, and will undermine your confidence in your own skills. They will criticize and reproach you off and on till you struggle to maintain your self-esteem. This happens to a lot of youngsters. Mama advises you to sever all connections with such people who constantly denigrate you. You deserve to be uplifted and encouraged because you are worthy and entirely capable of achieving your dreams. Do not let anyone ever tell you otherwise.

Sometimes, people may try to control you more subtly. They might even do it unconsciously. Here's what can happen. Some people in your life will try to 'help' you in your journey to attain your dreams. They will, perhaps with good intentions, try to assist you. However, their actions might just nudge you in a direction that you didn't want to take in the first place. If you aren't clear-sighted and certain enough, they can even take over your plan and leave you with little else, but directions to follow. Now, these people don't understand that you are the master of your own destiny. You are the author of your own story and can't play second fiddle to your own life.

So use your imaginary hula hoop to sever such people

from your life who hold you back and get in the way of your swaying momentum. Even the severing of some of these ties can be done in a smooth and delicate way, rather than abruptly or with anger. This applies to your family as well; even if they are restrictive, you have to be gentle at altering your ties with them.

So feel happy that you are being proactive about getting your rhythm and good vibes back. Mama is sure you want to feel free to work your way to your goals. Learn from the act of hula hooping and swing along in life with the confidence that you can keep the hoops going; just like the performers on the stage.

At Home In Your Hoop

You are the only person who can handle your hoops. So feel right at home in them; Mama says this so you understand that there is no one else who knows the hoops of your life like you do. Be confident and put your hoops around yourself; you can swing them with just the right energy and force. If you leave the task of twirling your hoops to others, you can very well end up with a hooping misadventure. How can anyone, other than you, control your hoops when they don't know what your hoop is all about? How can they keep your hoop moving, when they don't understand or know the way it needs to be handled? You, and everyone around you, are hula hooping their individual hoops in the best way they can. The metaphorical hoops that everyone has to swing are hard enough to handle, so, with all your own hoops to work with, how can you take on someone else's hoop and swing it successfully? Mama cautions against taking on other people's hoops just because you see them doing a mediocre or inadequate job at it. Just as no other person can continue your hula hooping act, you can't deal with their hula hoops either. Do not feel the need to get into someone else's hoop, though you may think you are qualified for it. You might end up creating a bigger mess than before, while also wasting your efforts. Learn the lesson of boundaries from this. Don't step into other's hoops and don't invite others to step into yours.

You have to make sure that the hoops you are working with belong in your life. You have to own them. Though you might be tempted to step out of your hoop because others' hoops look attractive, or you feel they need your help to keep going, Mama advises you to resist the temptation. The point of the hula hooping act is to get you to focus on your own hoops, and not on others'. Understand that if you try to get into another person's hoops, you will run into trouble. You can suggest to people on how to work their hoops and you can show them by example. But you can't do the hula hooping for them, just as they can't do it for you.

Sometimes, you will be assailed by fears of failing at your hula hooping act. Mama acknowledges that failure is inevitable, so you should never expect yourself to be one hundred percent successful at hula hooping, at least not in the beginning. Like other acts that you saw at the circus, hula hooping is something that you have to take your time to learn and master. So do not be deterred if the hoop falls down. It will fall down again and again, so just accept that fact. Instead of being disappointed, take your failure in stride and learn from it. Making mistakes is natural and expected while learning anything new. Before becoming a pro at this act, you will have to stumble and fall; take these as necessary lessons of hula hooping in life.

Mama would like you to know that sometimes success only comes after perceived failure. Use experiences, where you think you have failed, as stepping-stones. Think of it like this; every time you let the hula hoop fall down, you just find out one more way how not to do things. This is a part of gaining the experience you need to become better at managing your hoops. Be positive about the act and believe in yourself. The rest will follow. You will learn how to avoid errors and go around pitfalls, but this will only happen gradually. Do not rush the process. It will soon be programmed into your subconscious if you repeatedly convince yourself that you can make it. And you will. It is the power of suggestion through repetition that will definitely work for you.

In time, you will figure out the right rhythm with which to move with your hoops. Like Mama told you earlier, your hoops are made to fit you. You can even say that they are custom-made; exclusively for you. You will get the hang of successfully twirling them once you take their ownership and once you let yourself be yourself. You have to be who you really are and for this, you will have to disentangle from people and traditions that try to make you into someone you are not. Think about it yourself; if you let those external influences alter you, then will you fit into the hoops that are made for the real, authentic you? The answer is to never allow other things to take over your true self. You are equipped with all that you need to manage the hoops of your life and Mama wants you to never let anyone tell you otherwise.

Hooping Along

As you twirl your hula hoop, you will see many people around you do the same. You will run into some people who have the same or similar hoops as you do; in terms of hobbies or passions or any other hoop of life. When you find such people, you can hula hoop with them. You share some common ground so perhaps, you can also exchange tricks with each other on how to best manage the hoop. Practice your hula hooping with them and make the collaboration more productive by guiding each other and cheering each other on.

Mama doesn't mean for you to just hula hoop with like-minded people. In fact, Mama wants you to step out of your comfort zone and practice your hula hooping with different people who have different dreams and passions than you. Twirl with them as well because then, you can share your dreams with each other and broaden your perspective in the process. Take it as an adventure that you can go on. In fact, go on real adventures such as cross-country cycling! Expand your horizons. Once you do that, you might even discover a hidden talent for it. Then this will be a new addition to your hoops; one that you can work on slowly till you perfect it.

As you hula hoop with other people, the ones who are like you and the ones who are different, you will find out that there is a lot of value in those experiences that you share with other people. Not only will you learn about yourself, but you will also learn about other people and their passions. A whole new world will open up for you and your life will be all the more enriched for this. Be open to new experiences and always look for ways that you can improve and become better at managing the various hoops of your life.

While you twirl your many hula hoops, remember that sometimes you will have to let go of some hoops to better manage the other hoops. Sometimes, it will become necessary for you to let go of a hoop that has become a burden and that serves no real purpose in your life. Don't feel regretful and sad; just let that hoop fall with grace. Just understand that you will always have to deal with different hoops in different ways; some you will twirl for a long time and some you will have to let go earlier than expected. But don't take that as a failure, because sometimes, it is better to let go of a hoop than to stubbornly hold on to it. The point of hula hooping is not to take as many hoops as you can and twirl them around to the point of breakdown. It is to work well with the hoops that are aligned to your goal, for that is what will make for a happy and fun-filled time at the circus.

Hold The Hoops

"It's not the size of your hoop that matters. It's the authenticity of your flow."

- Erica R. Preston

So as you watched the hula hoop performance, you discovered so many things that you could learn from it. Mama was right beside you as you drew parallels between the act of hula hooping and your life. You learned how you have to manage several hoops in your life, which include your family, friends, work, as well as your worries and hobbies. This can be overwhelming. However, Mama knows that you now understand how to set your priorities when it comes to your hoops. You have learned that it is important to hold on to the hoops that matter and let go of the ones that don't.

Though you thought you controlled the hoops of your life, the hoops of your life in turn wield an influence over you. Therefore, it is imperative for you to get rid of the hoops that affect you negatively or hold you back. You also saw how hoops could be used to understand the concept of liberation. You learned that hula hooping through life can teach you to cut yourself off from all the things that restrain you. All in all, you were able to discover the various ways by which you can become better at managing the hula hoops of your life, by separating yourself from things that cause your hoop to crash to the ground.

Moreover, you understood how you can use your failures as lessons. You realized that it is important to take failures calmly and to not allow them to detract you from becoming better at hula hooping. You can now visualize your hoops and see that they really are made to fit only you. You cannot pass on your hoops to others to manage, nor can you control other people's hoops, though you might want to. You understand how that is a sure recipe for disaster. Your hoops are your own, and only you can handle them with the dexterity that is needed to keep the process going. You also learned that you will become better and more in sync with your hoops the more you practice. It is a fact that if you want to be successful and happy, you have to work with your own hoops, the ones of your own choice and the ones that are aligned with your dreams. You can also pair up with others who have similar hoops so you can have enriching life experiences. But then, you can also hula hoop with people who are unlike you so as to explore new possibilities and gain knowledge. This is your time to have adventures and to have fun. All throughout your experience of hula hooping, remember to remain true to yourself. This is the gist that Mama hopes you will take away from the circus. Be yourself fearlessly and in time, you will realize your dreams.

EPILOGUE

The circus of life never goes to sleep. Every moment that you spend here, you learn, you evolve, but most importantly, you become who you really are. Mama took you through the circus so you would grow. She held your hand and guided you through the acts of the circus, which is a metaphor for life, so you can transform. Mama hopes your trek through the circus has been illuminating, as well as entertaining, for that is what Mama believes to be the best way to learn in life.

You started your time in the circus with excitement. Before entering the circus tent, you waited in the queue and you learned all about the various queues of your life. As you arrived in the circus tent, you saw how several acts vied for your attention. You then understood that the circus of life is all about choices. Your decisions have the power to make it or break it for you. The acts that you went to were not just eye-catching performances, but they were invaluable life-lessons that made your journey worthwhile.

So you learned things from the clown, the acrobat, the circus dancers, the trapeze artists, the tightrope artists, and the jugglers. They all imparted valuable lessons to you, which most people miss out on because their eyes are not trained to delve beneath the surface. You, however, have understood to look beyond appearances. This is why even the circus music, the carousel, and the cotton candy, all taught you lessons, not only about the world around you, but about yourself. In the circus, even the trained animals served as a means of education for you. Isn't this something that not many can boast of?

Mama hopes that now, like a flower, you will flourish with the water and sunshine of knowledge imparted to you in this circus.

Mama also hopes that all her efforts will pay off when you implement everything you have learned from the circus to your life. Now, your time in this particular circus is ending, and you are ready to enter another queue. You are equipped with the right tools to make the best of it. So, Mama asks you, yet again, to become receptive to change. Open your mind and heart to receive the wisdom that will help you smoothly ride the rough and gentle waves of life.

Simplify things for yourself by outlining your goals and then working resolutely towards them. Believe wholeheartedly that you are fully capable of achieving your dreams. Mama stands with you, just as she did all through this circus journey. So fearlessly move ahead and go for the amazing life that awaits you. You have someone, in the image of Mama, to look to for guidance and encouragement. That, indeed, was the reason why Mama wrote this book.

So take flight, for you were meant to fly. You can color the skies with the shades of your choice. Reach higher and higher, because the stars that seemed so far away are within your grasp. All the inspiration that you seek outside of yourself lies within you. Mama hopes your time with her has been enriching. Once again, you will find Mama right by your side, cheering you on and taking your hand when you need help, because that is what mothers do.

CPSIA information can be obtained
at www.ICGtesting.com
Printed in the USA
BVHW080716020119
536773BV00016B/1483/P